it mylk

FROZEN YOGHURT

CONSTANCE and MATHILDE LORENZI

PHOTOGRAPHY by DAVID JAPY

STYLING by DA-RÔLE

MURDOCH BOOKS

Welcome to **our book**, where yoghurt is king. We love yoghurt so much that we gave up our jobs to start a company dedicated to it: **it mylk.** We opened our first **it mylk** shop in 2010, in the heart of Paris's sixth arondissement and we now have pop-up stores all around the city (the locations are on our website, www.itmylk.fr). We set ourselves a challenge in writing this book: to demonstrate in 61 recipes the reason for this divine madness ... While yoghurt has been the 'anti-dessert' for a long time — offered up in frustration when there's nothing else, the sad six-pack you take out of the refrigerator with a long face, apologising for not having made a *tart au chocolat* — for us it has become the essential ingredient in all the most cutting-edge desserts! At **it mylk**, we've chosen to take yoghurt to another level and show it off in all its guises. In this book not only will you learn how to make your own frozen yoghurts, but you'll also discover recipes for frozen yoghurt sandwiches, yoghurt combos, milkshakes and cakes based on our favourite ingredient. We are very happy to open the doors of our **it mylk** universe to you and wish you many happy hours making and eating your frozen yoghurts. Honesty obliges us to warn you, however, that frozen yoghurt is terribly addictive. Once you start ...

XxX

Constance & Mathilde Lorenzi

our

story

THE HISTORY OF FROZEN YOGHURT

THE VERY FIRST FROZEN YOGHURTS

Frozen yoghurt, called 'Frogurt' at that time, was invented in the 1970s in New England, in the United States, by H.P. Hood, an American company specialising in dairy products. In 1978, the Boston-based Brigham's restaurant chain (selling ice cream, sandwiches and candy) sold the first individually wrapped frozen yoghurt under the name Humphreez Yogart. At the same time, Dannon, the US subsidiary of the French Danone group, responded by creating Danny, a stick of frozen raspberry yoghurt coated in dark chocolate. But these products did not experience much success. For consumers at the time, even though the product was healthier than traditional ice cream it was still too much like traditional yoghurt, with an acidic flavour and not enough sweetness.

THE FIRST FROZEN YOGHURT CHAINS

In the 1980s, the first frozen yoghurt chains emerged in the United States, with a product that was sweeter and less bitter, with new recipes and new flavours that almost made you forget it was yoghurt. The Country's Best Yogurt (TCBY) and I Can't Believe It's Yogurt opened one outlet after another across America. The fad was launched, consumers being carried along by the fitness and diet food trends. Sales of frozen yoghurt increased by 200% between the middle of the 1980s and the early 1990s. By the end of the 1990s though, the craze had died down, and the traditional ice-cream brands launched their own lighter products in response, immediately making frozen yoghurt a less attractive option.

THE FROZEN YOGHURT WAVE IN THE USA

In the mid-2000s, a second frozen yoghurt wave swept the United States with the arrival of some big players who are still global market leaders today. In January 2005 the Pinkberry brand, launched by a pair of Korean Americans, Shelly Hwang and Young Lee, opened its first store in Los Angeles. It was an immediate hit, the word spreading thanks to American starlets like Paris Hilton. A permanent queue caused congestion in the area, which of course also fed the buzz. A second store opened in September 2006, and today there are more than 220 Pinkberry outlets all over the world. In 2007, South Korean brand Red Mango opened its first outlet in the United States. It now has 190 outlets worldwide.

FROZEN YOGHURT CONQUERS THE WORLD

Since 2010, frozen yoghurt has been on a path to world domination. Brands have multiplied in England, Germany, Spain, France and China, and frozen yoghurt has been carried along by the trends towards health foods and guilt-free pleasure. At the same time, brands are innovating and always offering more flavours and toppings. Soy milk, Greek-style yoghurt, goji berries, self-serve stores ... frozen yoghurt is being reinvented every day.

FROZEN YOGHURT FRENCH-STYLE

THE LOVE OF YOGHURT

Paris born and bred, we share two parents, an inordinate love for the café terraces of Saint-Germain-des-Prés, a funny little dog called Marcel and, above all, an uncontrollable addiction to yoghurt. Natural, with fruit, with white chocolate, stirred, as a drink or in a tub, during a break-up, a wedding or a detox, any excuse will do to bring out the little spoons!

FROM YOGHURT TO FROZEN YOGHURT

But we wanted to reinvent this yoghurt we loved, to bring it out of the fridge to make it THE new cutting-edge product ... We took the gamble, said goodbye to marketing and consulting firms and hello to New York in search of inspiration ... and the idea of frozen yoghurt French-style was born. The first **it mylk** shop opened in April 2010 in the heart of Paris's sixth arrondissement. Next came kiosks in Montmartre and at Charles de Gaulle Airport, a corner in a Paris department store and now we have lots of little pop-up food carts, which invade the capital as soon as spring is in the air ...

IT MYLK'S FROZEN YOGHURT

it mylk is a 0%-fat home-made frozen yoghurt, natural or flavoured, enjoyed with a selection of different toppings: fresh fruit, pieces of Isigny caramel, mini macarons, fruit compotes, crumble, granola ... The principle is simple: indulge yourself without guilt, with fresh products we've chosen with care, recipes made with passion and, above all, good yoghurt from the Viltain farm. **it mylk** is also a state of mind. Enjoying a frozen yoghurt is a way of reclaiming the forbidden frozen dessert. And since it's a lighter product, why not add little pieces of brownie, dulce de leche or white chocolate chips?

OTHER YOGHURT RECIPES

The **it mylk** universe is about yoghurt in all its glorious guises: frozen yoghurt of course, the cornerstone of the **it mylk** concept, but also frozen-yoghurt sandwiches, fresh yoghurts, milkshakes and desserts. In this book you will discover how to make frozen yoghurt at home using store-bought yoghurt: with an ice-cream maker, in five minutes with a blender, or even in the freezer, without any equipment at all. You will also learn how to make yoghurt in all its different forms and which ingredients to pair it with.

IT MYLK
A TALE OF YOGHURT

THE SEARCH FOR THE BEST YOGHURT

You can't develop a recipe for frozen yoghurt without a good yoghurt base. So before we opened our first store we set out on a veritable *tour de France* of yoghurt producers. This led us, after more than six months of searching, to the Viltain farm, where we finally discovered what we believed was the best yoghurt, fromage blanc and faisselle cheeses.

THE VILTAIN FARM

Located in Jouy-en-Josas, 17 kilometres (11 miles) from Paris, the Viltain farm divides its activities between growing grains and dairy farming. With a fresh food store, pick-your-own facilities (50 hectares/123 acres of fruit, vegetables and flowers), and a milking shed open to the public, it has always had a great sense of hospitality and innovation.

THE SECRET OF THE VILTAIN COWS

We only had to visit the Viltain farm once to understand the secret to such good yoghurt. It lies in the spa-quality treatment reserved for the establishment's 300 happy dairy cows. Pampered like Kobe cattle, they sleep on tatami mats and — the pinnacle of animal luxury — they have large electric-powered brushes in their stable that are triggered to scratch their backs when they walk underneath them!

TECHNICAL DETAILS: FROM THE COW TO THE YOGHURT

After the cows are milked, the milk is taken to the dairy, analysed for quality, then pasteurised, which is to say heated to 72°C (162°F) for 15 seconds. It is then cooled and heated back up to 43°C (109°F), and seeded by the introduction of two lactic acid bacteria, *Lactobacillus bulgaricus* and *Streptococcus thermophilus*. Finally, it is placed in sealed jars and sent to the hot room for three hours so the bacteria can multiply and turn the milk into yoghurt.

0%-FAT YOGHURT?

It's made from skim milk, so it has no fat. So we add a step in the process of transforming milk into yoghurt: the separation of the cream from the milk in a centrifugal separator.

THE STAR INGREDIENT: THE YOGHURT

GREEK YOGHURT

This is the ideal yoghurt for making frozen yoghurt at home! It is enriched with crème fraîche, giving it a particularly creamy texture. Traditionally, in Greece, it was made from sheep's milk and stored in small wooden or ceramic pots. It was an essential part of the shepherds' diet. Today in France, it's made from cow's milk. It contains nearly twice as much protein as a natural yoghurt, so it's very filling. As it's higher in fat, it's the fat-free version that gets our vote!

SHEEP'S MILK YOGHURT

Made from sheep's milk, a special feature of this very high-protein yoghurt is that it can be tolerated by those who can't tolerate cow's milk. So you can adapt all of the recipes in this book using sheep's milk yoghurt!

STIRRED YOGHURT

Unlike the fermentation process for firm or pot-set yoghurt, which takes place inside the tub, stirred yoghurt is fermented in vats before being blended. The only difference between these two yoghurts is how they're made. For frozen yoghurt, we prefer stirred yoghurt. But you get the same result from beating pot-set yoghurt.

FROMAGE BLANC

This fresh, unripened cheese is usually made from cow's milk. The percentage of dairy fat it contains depends on the type of milk used: full-cream, reduced-fat or skim milk. It is obtained by adding rennet and ferments to milk so it curdles. It is low in fat compared with other cheeses, and has a very mild flavour. **Petit-suisse** and **faisselle** are both yoghurt-like varieties of fresh cheese — smooth and creamy with neutral flavours. For the recipes in this book, fresh curd cheeses such as **quark** or even a thick **Greek yoghurt** can be used as substitutes in place of the varieties mentioned above. Alternatively, you can combine equal parts **cottage cheese** and **natural yoghurt**, and mix together until smooth.

IT MYLK'S HEALTHY INGREDIENTS

AGAVE SYRUP

This natural sweetener is the sweet nectar of a Mexican cactus, the blue or tequila agave. Once filtered, heated and hydrolysed, the resulting syrup resembles honey. Mainly made up of fructose (the natural sugar in fruit), it has a low glycaemic index, which means it can be tolerated by certain types of diabetics. Meanwhile, its powerful sweetening ability reduces the amount of sugar needed. While it was already well known to the Aztecs, who gave it as an offering to their gods, its neutral taste, nutritional qualities and sweetening properties have made it an easy-to-use weight-loss ally.

OAT BRAN

Oat bran, the outer layer of the oat grain, has become the star cereal of diets. High in the soluble fibre that absorbs fats in the stomach and carbohydrates from other foods eaten at the same time, oat bran helps reduce the intake of kilojoules. It also absorbs up to thirty times its volume in water, meaning it quickly creates a sensation of fullness when eaten during a meal. Healthwise, it helps to reduce cholesterol and prevent colon cancer. Recommended dose: a maximum of 2 tablespoons per person per day.

SPIRULINA

A blue-green microalgae more than 3 billion years old with unprecedented nutritional and therapeutic benefits, spirulina is mainly found naturally in India, Mexico and Africa. It is sold in powder and tablet form. It contains high-quality proteins, omega 6, minerals and trace elements. It is a concentrated energy source recommended for athletes. Healthwise, it is supposed to combat the ageing process, strengthen the immune system, slow down hair loss …

YUZU

Irregularly shaped and green or yellow depending on its maturity, this small citrus fruit is native to East Asia. It is filled with seeds, but its highly aromatic zest and juice are widely used in Japanese cuisine. High in vitamin C and recommended for rheumatism and high cholesterol, it offers undeniable health benefits. In terms of wellbeing, its essential oil is used in baths for its relaxing and soothing properties. As a massage oil, it is even said that it makes cellulite disappear!

KALE

Also called curly kale and borecole, kale is the only cabbage that doesn't form a head but grows in long stems covered with deep green curly leaves. It was very popular in the Middle Ages, and is making a real health-food comeback on our plates today. High in nutrients, antioxidants and fibre and very low in kilojoules, kale is a real nutritional bombshell. It can be eaten raw or cooked, in a salad or as a side-dish, in soups, quiches, juices …

LINSEED

Linseed comes from flax, an annual plant grown in temperate and tropical climates. Its seeds are so prized today because of their high levels of plant-based omega 3. Important note: the seeds need to be ground for the body to benefit, otherwise they only act as a form of dietary fibre for digestion. Healthwise, linseed is said to reduce the risk of breast and colon cancer, and strengthen the immune system. Its subtle nutty flavour goes well with pancakes, fruit salad, yoghurt …

THE TOOLS FOR HOME-MADE FROZEN YOGHURT

ICE-CREAM MAKER

Two types of ice-cream makers can be used to make frozen yoghurt: cold-accumulating or self-powered. Whatever the model, the principle is fairly simple. Pour the mixture into the ice-cream maker and churn for 20–30 minutes, depending on the power of the churn and the amount of frozen yoghurt. For a more solid texture, frozen yoghurt can be put in the freezer after it's made until it has the desired consistency.

— Cold-accumulating ice-cream makers

The price makes these more accessible than self-powered ice-cream makers, and they can be found in all kitchen appliance stores. As they do not generate cold, the cold-accumulating bowl needs to be put in the freezer for 12 hours before use.

— Self-powered ice-cream makers

Usually reserved for professionals, these are more expensive and cumbersome, but don't require any lead-time before freezing and give you the option of making several frozen yoghurt recipes in a row.

FREEZER

You can make frozen yoghurt at home without an ice-cream maker. Just put your mixture in an airtight freezer-safe container, seal it and let it set for about 4 hours (again, the time depends on the power of the freezer and the amount of frozen yoghurt made). ✳ It is imperative, however, that you take the mixture out of the freezer every hour to whip it. This step is essential to prevent the formation of ice crystals and ensure an airy texture.

THE BLENDER (INSTANT FROZEN YOGHURT!)

A trick for making home-made frozen yoghurt without an ice-cream maker and in 5 minutes is to use frozen fruit and a blender. The principle is simple: blend frozen fruit with your yoghurt mixture. ✳ Make sure you don't take the fruit out of the freezer until the last minute, so it stays well frozen. If you have time, put the yoghurt in the freezer for 15 minutes before starting the recipe. Don't over-blend, so you have a smooth mixture that still has a frozen consistency. For a firmer consistency, transfer the frozen yoghurt to a suitable container and leave in the freezer for 1 hour. You can also freeze fruit yourself: just cut it into chunks, place it in an airtight container suitable for the freezer, and let the fruit freeze for about 4 hours.

✳ *Frozen yoghurt recipes pages 24 and 26.*

PRESENTATION AND DECORATION

PRESENTATION

— Soft-serve (it mylk-style)

Tool: piping (icing) bag fitted with a star nozzle.
Container: small wide-topped cup or small coloured
cupcake case, to decorate with a topping.
Process: put the piping bag in the freezer for
1 hour before use. Be careful when you're ready to
pipe: it's cold, very cold; feel free to wear gloves!

— Scoop (classic-style)

Tool: ice-cream scoop.
Container: small bowl or plate.
Process: vary the size of the scoops. Feel free to
make mini scoops using a melon baller ... and even
mini scoop kebabs using wooden skewers.

— Quenelles (foodie-style)

Tool: two large spoons.
Container: plate.
Process: take the frozen yoghurt out of the freezer
15 minutes before serving to let it soften a little and make
it easier to work with. Using two large spoons, form
quenelles by transferring the frozen mixture from one
spoon to the other, smoothing the surface at the same
time. For especially smooth quenelles, dip the two spoons
in hot water and give the surface of the quenelles a final
smoothing over before serving.
Tip: for the less adventurous, there are quenelle-shaped
ice-cream scoops.

DECORATING IDEAS

— Fun flags

Tools: toothpicks + decorative adhesive tape + scissors.
1. Cut a 5 cm (2 inch) strip of decorative tape.
2. Place a toothpick in the centre of the strip.
3. Fold over and stick together the two sides of the strip.
4. Cut out a V-shape at the end of the strip of tape.
5. Plant the small flag in the cake or frozen yoghurt.

— Straws with a twist

For plunging into a milkshake.
Tools: drinking straw + decorative adhesive tape + scissors.
1. Cover a traditional straw with decorative tape,
   wrapped around on the diagonal.
2. Trim the pieces of tape that hang over the
   ends of the straw.
3. Insert the decorated straw into the milkshake.

frozen yoghurts

NATURAL FROZEN YOGHURT

NATURAL FROZEN YOGHURT

makes 6 frozen yoghurts • preparation time
5 minutes • freezing time 25 minutes

500 g (1 lb 2 oz) STIRRED YOGHURT
75 g (2½ oz/⅓ cup) SUGAR
200 ml (7 fl oz) THIN (POURING) CREAM
equipment ICE-CREAM MAKER, ELECTRIC BEATER

METHOD

Whisk the yoghurt and sugar together until the sugar
has completely dissolved. Beat the cream in a separate
bowl with the electric beater to thicken it, then add the
yoghurt and sugar mixture. Whisk together. Pour the
mixture into an ice-cream maker and churn for about
25 minutes.

FREEZER OPTION

Make the same mixture, place in a freezer-safe airtight
container and close with a lid. Let the mixture set in the
freezer for about 4 hours (the time depends on the power
of the freezer and the amount of frozen yoghurt made).
Take the mixture out of the freezer every hour and beat
using the electric beater. This step is essential to prevent
ice crystals forming and to ensure an airy texture.

0%-FAT FROZEN YOGHURT

makes 6 frozen yoghurts • preparation time
5 minutes • freezing time 25 minutes

500 g (1 lb 2 oz) FAT-FREE POT-SET GREEK YOGHURT
50 ml (1½ fl oz) AGAVE SYRUP
2 TABLESPOONS SKIM MILK
½ LEMON, JUICED
equipment ICE-CREAM MAKER, ELECTRIC BEATER

METHOD

Whisk the yoghurt and agave syrup together until
frothy. Add the milk and lemon juice, and mix again.
Pour the mixture into an ice-cream maker and churn
for about 25 minutes.

FREEZER OPTION

Make the same mixture, place in a freezer-safe airtight
container and close with a lid. Let the mixture set in the
freezer for about 4 hours (the time depends on the power
of the freezer and the amount of frozen yoghurt made).
Take the mixture out of the freezer every hour and beat
using the electric beater. This step is essential to prevent
ice crystals forming and to ensure an airy texture.

MARCEL'S SHOPPING TIP: WHERE TO FIND 0%-FAT GREEK YOGHURT

*Fat-free pot-set Greek yoghurt is available from speciality food stores and in some
supermarkets. You can also substitute fat-free stirred yoghurt, but the texture will
not be as creamy ...*

FLAVOURED FROZEN YOGHURT

0%-FAT STRAWBERRY

makes 6 frozen yoghurts • preparation time 10 minutes • churning time 25 minutes

500 g (1 lb 2 oz) FAT-FREE GREEK YOGHURT, 500 g (1 lb 2 oz) STRAWBERRIES, 50 ml (1½ fl oz) AGAVE SYRUP,
equipment ICE-CREAM MAKER, BLENDER

METHOD

Wash and hull the strawberries and purée them in a blender. Combine the strawberries and agave syrup in a bowl, add the yoghurt and whisk until the mixture is smooth. Pour into an ice-cream maker and churn for about 25 minutes.

0%-FAT VANILLA

makes 6 frozen yoghurts • preparation time 5 minutes • churning time 25 minutes

500 g (1 lb 2 oz) FAT-FREE GREEK OR STIRRED YOGHURT, 3 EGGS, PINCH FINE SALT, 75 g (2½ oz/ ⅓ cup) SUGAR (OR 1½ TABLESPOONS SWEETENER), 1 VANILLA BEAN, SEEDS SCRAPED
equipment ICE-CREAM MAKER, ELECTRIC BEATER

METHOD

Separate the egg whites and yolks. Beat the egg whites to soft peaks with salt. Beat the egg yolks and sugar in a separate bowl until the mixture is pale. Add the vanilla seeds, then fold in the egg whites using a spatula. Fold in the yoghurt. Pour the mixture into an ice-cream maker and churn for about 25 minutes.

✳ *Salidou is a French brand of salted butter caramel spread. Use a good-quality equivalent from a speciality food store or delicatessen if you can't track it down.*

SALIDOU

makes 6 frozen yoghurts • preparation time 5 minutes • churning time 25 minutes

500 g (1 lb 2 oz) STIRRED YOGHURT, 55 g (2 oz/¼ cup) SUGAR, 200 ml (7 fl oz) THIN (POURING) CREAM, 150 g (5½ oz) SALIDOU ✳ SALTED BUTTER CARAMEL SPREAD (OR THICK CARAMEL SAUCE), 1 VANILLA BEAN, SEEDS SCRAPED
equipment ICE-CREAM MAKER, ELECTRIC BEATER

METHOD

Mix the yoghurt and sugar together until the sugar has dissolved. Beat the cream in a spearate bowl with the electric beater to thicken it, then add the yoghurt and sugar mixture. Whisk together. Add the salted butter caramel spread, and the vanilla seeds, and whisk until the mixture is smooth. Pour into an ice-cream maker and churn for about 25 minutes.

CHOCOLATE

makes 6 frozen yoghurts • preparation time 15 minutes • refrigeration time 1 hour • churning time 25 minutes

500 g (1 lb 2 oz) GREEK YOGHURT, 120 g (4¼ oz) DARK CHOCOLATE, BROKEN INTO PIECES, 110 g (3¾ oz/ ½ cup) SUGAR, 30 g (1 oz/¼ cup) COCOA POWDER, 125 ml (4 fl oz/½ cup) THIN (POURING) CREAM
equipment ICE-CREAM MAKER

METHOD

Melt the chocolate in a double boiler over a low heat. Stir to dissolve the sugar and melt the chocolate. Off the heat, sift over the cocoa powder and whisk in until smooth. Add the cream and yoghurt, whisk until the mixture is smooth and set aside for 1 hour in the refrigerator. Pour the mixture into an ice-cream maker and churn for about 25 minutes.

frozen yoghurts

TOPPINGS

GRANOLA

makes 300 g (10½ oz) • preparation time 10 minutes • cooking time 20 to 30 minutes

100 g (3½ oz/1 cup) ROLLED (PORRIDGE) OATS, 25 g (1 oz/¼ cup) BARLEY OATS, 40 g (1½ oz/¼ cup) CHOPPED ALMONDS, 35 g (1¼ oz/¼ cup) CHOPPED HAZELNUTS, 3 TABLESPOONS HONEY, 1 TABLESPOON SUNFLOWER OIL, 1 TEASPOON GROUND CINNAMON, 30 g (1 oz) RAISINS

METHOD

Combine all the ingredients except the raisins. Spread the mixture over a baking tray lined with baking paper, and place in a 150°C (300°F/Gas 2) oven. Stir every 10 minutes until browned (about 20–30 minutes). Allow to cool, add the raisins and mix.

CRUMBLE

makes 300 g (10½ oz) • preparation time 15 minutes • cooking time 15 minutes

75 g (2½ oz) UNSALTED BUTTER, SOFTENED, 75 g (2½ oz/⅓ cup) CASTER (SUPERFINE) SUGAR, 75 g (2½ oz/½ cup) PLAIN (ALL-PURPOSE) FLOUR, 70 g (2½ oz/⅔ cup) ALMOND MEAL

METHOD

Line a baking tray with baking paper. Work the butter and sugar together with your fingertips. Add the flour and almond meal, then work with your hands to make a crumbly mixture. Refrigerate for 10 minutes. Spread the mixture over the tray and bake at 200°C (400°F/Gas 6) for 15 minutes.

APPLE COMPOTE

makes 300 g (10½ oz) • preparation time 10 minutes • cooking time 20 minutes

2 LARGE APPLES, PEELED, CORED AND CHOPPED, 45 g (1¾ oz/¼ cup) BROWN SUGAR, 2 TABLESPOONS WARM WATER

METHOD

Cook the ingredients in a covered saucepan over a low heat for 20 minutes, stirring from time to time until the apple is cooked and softened.

INDULGENT TOPPINGS

CHOCOLATE TOPPINGS

Chocolate peeled with a vegetable peeler (white, dark, milk, praline ...), a dollop of chocolate spread, crumbled chocolate biscuits ...

BISCUIT TOPPINGS

Home-made cake cut into cubes (madeleines, loaf cakes ...), crumbled store-bought biscuits ...

LOLLY TOPPINGS

Lolly (candy) mixes (strawberries, crocodiles ...).

LIGHT TOPPINGS

CEREAL/DRIED FRUIT + NUT TOPPINGS

Breakfast cereals, roughly chopped walnuts, almonds, hazelnuts or pecans, dried fruit from the cupboard (cranberries, dried bananas, desiccated coconut ...).

FRESH FRUIT TOPPINGS

Seasonal fruits cut into pieces: strawberry, kiwi fruit, mango ...

MARCEL'S SECRET TREATS

The granola will keep in an airtight jar and can be made in large quantities!
Variations: 20 g (¾ oz) dried banana chips, coconut shavings, dried cranberries, chocolate chips or caramelised pecans ...
Fruit compote variations: strawberry–rhubarb, pear, mango–coconut ...

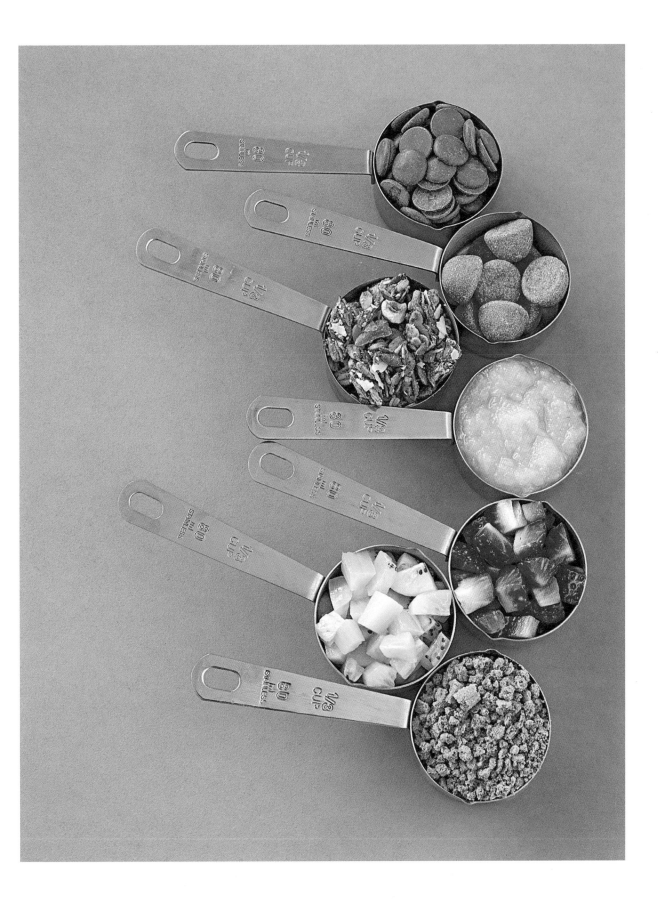

SAUCES AND COULIS

CHOCOLATE SAUCE

makes 500 g (1 lb 2 oz) sauce, or 6 servings • preparation time 10 minutes

2 TABLESPOONS THIN (POURING) CREAM, 200 ml (7 fl oz) MILK, 200 g (7 oz) DARK CHOCOLATE, 40 g (1½ oz) UNSALTED BUTTER, 2 TABLESPOONS SUGAR

METHOD

Heat the cream and milk over a low heat. Remove the saucepan from the heat before the mixture comes to the boil. Add the chocolate, in pieces, and stir until melted. Add the butter and sugar and heat, stirring, until the mixture is smooth.

DULCE DE LECHE

makes 500 g (1 lb 2 oz) sauce, or 6 servings • preparation time 10 minutes • cooking time 1 hour

1 litre (35 fl oz/4 cups) FULL-CREAM MILK, 330 g (11½ oz/1½ cups) CASTER (SUPERFINE) SUGAR, 1 TEASPOON BICARBONATE OF SODA (BAKING SODA), 1 VANILLA BEAN, 1 PINCH FINE SEA SALT

METHOD

Put all the ingredients into a saucepan and heat over a high heat, stirring constantly. When the milk begins to colour, reduce the heat to medium and continue cooking and stirring until the sauce reaches the desired consistency and colour. Remove the vanilla bean. Stop the cooking process by placing the saucepan into a larger saucepan of cold water or by pouring the sauce into jars.

RASPBERRY COULIS

makes 500 g (1 lb 2 oz) coulis, or 6 servings • preparation time 10 minutes • cooling time 1 hour

500 g (1 lb 2 oz) RASPBERRIES, 125 ml (4 fl oz/½ cup) AGAVE SYRUP, 2 TABLESPOONS LEMON JUICE

METHOD

Rinse the raspberries and place them in a saucepan with the agave syrup and lemon juice. Bring to the boil, stirring with a wooden spoon. Remove from the heat and pass the sauce through a fine sieve to remove the small raspberry seeds. Cool the sauce in the refrigerator.

INSTANT STRAWBERRY COULIS

makes 500 g (1 lb 2 oz) coulis, or 6 servings • preparation time 5 minutes

500 g (1 lb 2 oz) STRAWBERRIES, 2 TABLESPOONS SUGAR, BALSAMIC VINEGAR

METHOD

Wash and hull the strawberries, then place them in a blender with the sugar and a dash of balsamic vinegar. Blend until smooth. To make the sauce even smoother, pass it through a fine sieve.

FROZEN GRANOLA
NATURAL BASE + GRANOLA TOPPING

makes 6 frozen yoghurts
preparation time 15 minutes
cooking time 20 to 30 minutes

800 g (1 lb 12 oz) NATURAL FROZEN YOGHURT ✳

granola
100 g (3½ oz/1 cup) ROLLED (PORRIDGE) OATS
25 g (1 oz/¼ cup) BARLEY OATS
40 g (1½ oz/¼ cup) CHOPPED ALMONDS
30 g (1 oz/¼ cup) CHOPPED HAZELNUTS
3 TABLESPOONS HONEY
1 TABLESPOON SUNFLOWER OIL
1 TEASPOON GROUND CINNAMON
1 PINCH SALT
2 TABLESPOONS RAISINS

fresh fruit
2 BANANAS
200 g (7 oz) STRAWBERRIES (OR OTHER FRUIT
OF YOUR CHOICE: KIWI FRUIT, APPLES ...)

equipment
PIPING (ICING) BAG AND STAR NOZZLE

✳ *The recipe for this is on page 24.*

PREPARATION
Place the piping bag and nozzle in the freezer for a few minutes so they are well chilled.

GRANOLA
Line a baking tray with a sheet of baking paper. Combine all the ingredients together except the raisins. Spread the mixture over the baking tray and slide it into the oven. Set the oven temperature to 150°C (300°F/Gas 2) and bake the granola, watching it closely and mixing every 10 minutes until it reaches the desired colour (20–30 minutes, depending on the oven). Allow to cool, add the raisins and mix.

FRESH FRUIT
Peel the bananas and slice them into rounds. Wash and hull the strawberries and cut them into quarters lengthways.

ASSEMBLY
If the frozen yoghurt was made ahead of time, take it out of the freezer 10 minutes before piping to make it more malleable. Using a spatula, fill the piping bag (nozzle attached) with yoghurt. Pipe out the frozen yoghurt soft-serve style into six serving bowls, then scatter over the granola and fresh fruit. Serve immediately.

FROZEN TATIN
NATURAL BASE + TARTE TATIN TOPPING

makes 6 frozen yoghurts
preparation time 15 minutes
cooling time 10 minutes
cooking time 35 minutes

800 g (1 lb 12 oz) NATURAL FROZEN YOGHURT ✳

apple compote
2 LARGE APPLES (GRANNY SMITH, BELLE
DE BOSKOOP, GOLDEN RUSSET, REINE DES
REINETTES)
45 g (1¾ oz/¼ cup) LIGHT BROWN SUGAR
2 TABLESPOONS LUKEWARM WATER

crumble
75 g (2½ oz) UNSALTED BUTTER, AT ROOM
TEMPERATURE
75 g (2½ oz/⅓ cup) CASTER (SUPERFINE) SUGAR
75 g (2½ oz/½ cup) PLAIN (ALL-PURPOSE)
WHOLEMEAL (WHOLEWHEAT) FLOUR
70 g (2½ oz/⅔ cup) ALMOND MEAL

equipment
PIPING (ICING) BAG AND STAR NOZZLE

✳ *The recipe for this is on page 24.*

PREPARATION
Place the piping bag and nozzle in the freezer for a few minutes
so they are well chilled.

APPLE COMPOTE
Peel and core the apples and cut into chunks. Place them in a
saucepan with the brown sugar and water. Cover and cook over
a low heat for about 20 minutes, stirring from time to time with a
wooden spoon. Stop cooking when you can easily crush the apples
with the spoon.

CRUMBLE
Work the butter and sugar together with your fingertips. Add the
flour and almond meal, then work together with your hands to
make a crumbly mixture. Refrigerate for 10 minutes, then spread
the mixture over a baking tray lined with baking paper and bake at
200°C (400°F/Gas 6) for 15 minutes. Leave to cool.

ASSEMBLY
If the frozen yoghurt was made ahead of time, take it out of the
freezer 10 minutes before piping to make it more malleable. Place
1–2 tablespoons of compote in each serving bowl. Using a spatula,
fill the piping bag (nozzle attached), and pipe out the yoghurt soft-
serve style. Sprinkle with crumble and serve immediately.

MARCEL'S LAZY SHORTCUT

*Replace the home-made crumble with store-bought shortbread biscuits,
coarsely crumbled.*

FROZEN STRAWBERRY TART
NATURAL BASE + STRAWBERRY TART TOPPING

makes 6 frozen yoghurts
preparation time 15 minutes
resting time 30 minutes
cooking time 10 minutes

800 g (1 lb 12 oz) NATURAL FROZEN YOGHURT ✳

strawberry filling
250 g (9 oz) STRAWBERRIES, HULLED
1 TABLESPOON CRUSHED PISTACHIOS

biscuits
1 EGG
55 g (2 oz/¼ cup) CASTER (SUPERFINE) SUGAR
200 g (7 oz/1⅓ cups) PLAIN (ALL-PURPOSE) FLOUR
75 g (2½ oz) UNSALTED BUTTER, SOFTENED

equipment
PIPING (ICING) BAG AND STAR NOZZLE
8 cm (3¼ inch) ROUND CUTTER

✳ *The recipe for this is on page 24.*

PREPARATION
Place the piping bag and nozzle in the freezer for a few minutes so they are well chilled.

BISCUITS
Preheat the oven to 180°C (350°F/Gas 4). Whisk the egg with the sugar. Gradually add the sifted flour and the butter. Work together with your fingertips to make a smooth dough. Roll it out on a sheet of baking paper and let it firm in the refrigerator for 30 minutes, then cut into six 8 cm (3¼ inch) rounds. Place them on a baking tray lined with baking paper and bake for 10 minutes, then cool on the baking tray.

STRAWBERRY FILLING
Wash the strawberries and cut them into rounds.

ASSEMBLY
If the frozen yoghurt was made ahead of time, take it out of the freezer 10 minutes before piping to make it more malleable. Using a spatula, fill the piping bag (nozzle attached) with yoghurt. Place a biscuit on a plate, cover with slices of strawberry, then pipe on a rosette of the frozen yoghurt. Scatter with crushed pistachios and serve immediately.

MARCEL'S DECORATING TIP

Make the strawberries shiny by brushing them with melted strawberry jelly.

FROZEN LEMON PIE
NATURAL BASE + LEMON PIE TOPPING

makes 6 frozen yoghurts
preparation time 30 minutes
cooling time 30 minutes
cooking time 1 hour 45 minutes

800 g (1 lb 12 oz) NATURAL FROZEN YOGHURT ✳

lemon curd
185 ml (6 fl oz/¾ cup) LEMON JUICE
3 EGGS
1 TABLESPOON CORNFLOUR (CORNSTARCH)
200 ml (7 fl oz) AGAVE SYRUP

meringues
2 EGG WHITES
140 g (5 oz/⅔ cup) SUGAR

crumble
40 g (1½ oz) UNSALTED BUTTER,
AT ROOM TEMPERATURE
2 TABLESPOONS CASTER (SUPERFINE) SUGAR
35 g (1¼ oz/¼ cup) WHOLEMEAL (WHOLEWHEAT)
FLOUR
35 g (1¼ oz/⅓ cup) ALMOND MEAL

equipment
2 PIPING (ICING) BAGS, 1 STAR NOZZLE
AND 1 SMALL PLAIN NOZZLE

✳ *The recipe for this is on page 24.*

PREPARATION
Place a piping bag and the star nozzle in the freezer for a few minutes so they are well chilled.

LEMON CURD
Bring the lemon juice to a bare simmer in a saucepan, then turn off the heat. Whisk the eggs with the cornflour and agave syrup in a bowl until the mixture is smooth. Pour into the saucepan and thicken over medium heat, stirring constantly with a wooden spoon. Allow to cool in the refrigerator for 30 minutes.

MERINGUES
Whisk the egg whites to firm peaks with half the sugar. Add the remaining sugar and mix gently. Line a baking tray with baking paper. Using a tablespoon, place small mounds of meringue mixture on the tray, spaced far enough apart so they don't stick together. Bake for 20 minutes at 120°C (235°F/Gas ½), then 1 hour at 100°C (200°F/Gas ½). Once the meringues have cooled, break them into pieces.

CRUMBLE
Work the butter and sugar together with your fingertips. Add the flour and almond meal, then work together to make a crumbly mixture. Refrigerate for 10 minutes, then spread the mixture on a baking tray and bake at 200°C (400°F/Gas 6) for 15 minutes.

ASSEMBLY
If the frozen yoghurt is in the freezer, take it out 10 minutes ahead of time. Fill the cold piping bag (star nozzle attached) with yoghurt. Pipe out the yoghurt soft-serve style and sprinkle with the broken meringue and the crumble. Pipe small balls of lemon curd onto the frozen yoghurt with the other piping bag (plain nozzle attached). Serve immediately.

MARCEL'S TIPS

Replace the home-made meringues with store-bought mini meringues. You can keep the extra curd in an airtight container for 3–4 days in the refrigerator.

FROZEN YUZU
NATURAL BASE + YUZU CURD TOPPING

makes 6 frozen yoghurts
preparation time 20 minutes
cooking time 20 minutes
resting & cooling time 45 minutes

800 g (1 lb 12 oz) NATURAL FROZEN YOGHURT ✳

biscuits
1 EGG
55 g (2 oz/¼ cup) CASTER (SUPERFINE) SUGAR
200 g (7 oz/1⅓ cups) PLAIN (ALL-PURPOSE) FLOUR
75 g (2½ oz) UNSALTED BUTTER, SOFTENED

yuzu curd
150 ml (5 fl oz) BOTTLE YUZU JUICE (AVAILABLE
FROM JAPANESE FOOD STORES)
3 EGGS
1 TABLESPOON CORNFLOUR (CORNSTARCH)
200 ml (7 fl oz) AGAVE SYRUP

equipment
PIPING (ICING) BAG AND STAR NOZZLE
FLUTED CUTTER

✳ *The recipe for this is on page 24.*

PREPARATION
Place the piping bag and nozzle in the freezer for a few minutes
so they are well chilled.

BISCUITS
Preheat the oven to 180°C (350°F/Gas 4). Whisk the egg with the
sugar, then gradually add the flour and the softened butter. Work
the mixture together with your fingertips to make a smooth dough.
Roll it out on a sheet of baking paper, then let it firm up in the
refrigerator for 30 minutes. Cut out shapes using a fluted cutter.
Place on a baking tray lined with baking paper and bake for
10 minutes, then cool on the baking tray.

YUZU CURD
Bring the yuzu juice to a bare simmer in a saucepan, then turn off the
heat. Whisk the eggs with the cornflour and agave syrup in a bowl
until the mixture is smooth, with no lumps. Pour it into the saucepan
and thicken over medium heat, stirring constantly with a wooden
spoon. Remove from the heat and allow to cool.

ASSEMBLY
If the frozen yoghurt is in the freezer, take it out 10 minutes ahead
of time. Using a spatula, fill the piping bag (nozzle attached) with
yoghurt. Divide the yuzu curd between six small serving bowls, pipe
over the frozen yoghurt soft-serve style and decorate with the halved
biscuit. Garnish with grated citrus zest if desired. Serve immediately.

MARCEL'S LAZY SHORTCUT

Replace the home-made biscuits with store-bought biscuits.

FROZEN HOT CHOCOLATE
NATURAL BASE + HOT CHOCOLATE TOPPING

makes 6 frozen yoghurts
preparation time 10 minutes
cooking time 10 minutes

800 g (1 lb 12 oz) NATURAL FROZEN YOGHURT ✳

old-style hot chocolate
400 ml (14 fl oz) MILK
200 ml (7 fl oz) WATER
150 ml (5 fl oz) THIN (POURING) CREAM
2 TABLESPOONS SUGAR
30 g (1 oz/¼ cup) COCOA POWDER
200 g (7 oz) DARK CHOCOLATE
6 TABLESPOONS MINI MARSHMALLOWS

equipment
PIPING (ICING) BAG AND STAR NOZZLE

✳ *The recipe for this is on page 24.*

PREPARATION
Place the piping bag and nozzle in the freezer for a few minutes so they are well chilled.

HOT CHOCOLATE
Heat the milk, water and cream in a saucepan without letting them boil. Mix in the sugar and cocoa powder. Roughly chop the chocolate and place in a bowl. Pour over the hot chocolate milk and mix with a spatula until smooth. Pour the mixture into the saucepan and thicken over medium heat, stirring constantly so the chocolate doesn't catch.

ASSEMBLY
If the frozen yoghurt is in the freezer, take it out 10 minutes ahead of time. Using a spatula, fill the piping bag (nozzle attached) with yoghurt. Divide the hot chocolate between six small serving bowls, pipe the frozen yoghurt on top, soft-serve style, and scatter over the mini marshmallows. Serve immediately.

FROZEN PEACH SAUTÉ

NATURAL BASE + PEACH TOPPING

makes 6 frozen yoghurts
preparation time 15 minutes
cooking time 15 minutes
cooling time 20 minutes

800 g (1 lb 12 oz) NATURAL FROZEN YOGHURT ✳

sautéed peaches with rosemary
5 PEACHES
1 TEASPOON BUTTER
60 ml (2 fl oz/¼ cup) AGAVE SYRUP
2 ROSEMARY SPRIGS

equipment
PIPING (ICING) BAG AND STAR NOZZLE

✳ *The recipe for this is on page 24.*

· PREPARATION
Place the piping bag and nozzle in the freezer for a few minutes so they are well chilled.

SAUTÉED PEACHES WITH ROSEMARY
Peel the peaches and cut them into segments. Heat the butter in a frying pan over medium heat. When it has melted, add the agave syrup and let it caramelise. Add the peach segments and rosemary sprigs. Cook over a medium heat for 3–4 minutes, shaking the frying pan regularly. Remove from the heat and allow to cool in the refrigerator for 20 minutes, then remove the rosemary.

ASSEMBLY
Divide the peach between six small serving glasses. If the frozen yoghurt is in the freezer, take it out 10 minutes ahead of time. Using a spatula, fill the piping bag (nozzle attached) with yoghurt, and pipe it out soft-serve style on top of the peaches. Serve immediately.

MARCEL'S EXTRAS

You can replace the agave syrup with rosemary honey for even more flavour. If you're a fan of berries, add 200 g (7 oz) quartered strawberries to the peaches for the last minute of cooking.

FROZEN CRÈME BRÛLÉE
VANILLA BASE + CRÈME BRÛLÉE TOPPING

makes 6 frozen yoghurts
preparation time 15 minutes
cooking time 10 minutes

800 g (1 lb 12 oz) VANILLA FROZEN YOGHURT ✳
300 g (10½ oz) WHOLE BERRIES, SUCH AS
RASPBERRIES OR BLUEBERRIES (OPTIONAL)

crème brûlée topping
55 g (2 oz/¼ cup) RAW (DEMERARA) SUGAR
1 TEASPOON ORANGE LIQUEUR
1 CLOVE

equipment
SMALL FOOD PROCESSOR
PIPING (ICING) BAG AND STAR NOZZLE

✳ *The recipe for this is on page 26.*

PREPARATION

Place the piping bag and nozzle in the freezer for a few minutes
so they are well chilled.

CRÈME BRÛLÉE TOPPING

Put the sugar, liqueur and clove in the bowl of the food processor
and process until the sugar has completely blended with the liqueur.
Line a baking tray with baking paper. Spread the sugar over the tray
and bake at 200°C (400°F/Gas 6) for about 10 minutes. Keep a close
eye on it: the mixture mustn't burn. Let it cool for a few minutes,
then break the resulting sheets of sugar into small pieces.

ASSEMBLY

If the frozen yoghurt is in the freezer, take it out 10 minutes ahead
of time. Using a spatula, fill the piping bag (nozzle attached) with
yoghurt. Pipe out the frozen yoghurt soft-serve style into six small
serving dishes, then decorate with the crème brûlée topping and
whole berries, if using. Serve immediately.

FROZEN SALIDOU AND CHOUCHOUS
SALTED BUTTER CARAMEL BASE + TOFFEED PEANUT TOPPING

makes 6 frozen yoghurts
preparation time 10 minutes
cooking time about 1 hour
cooling time 20 minutes

800 g (1 lb 12 oz) SALIDOU FROZEN YOGHURT ✳

chouchous (toffeed peanuts)
250 ml (9 fl oz/1 cup) WATER
140 g (5 oz/1 cup) UNSALTED PEANUTS,
IN THEIR SKINS
220 g (7¾ oz/1 cup) SUGAR

equipment
PIPING (ICING) BAG AND STAR NOZZLE

✳ *The recipe for this is on page 26. Salidou is a French brand of salted butter caramel spread. Use a good-quality equivalent from a speciality food store or delicatessen if you can't track it down.*

PREPARATION

Place the piping bag and nozzle in the freezer for a few minutes so they are well chilled.

CHOUCHOUS

Bring the water to the boil with the peanuts and sugar in a saucepan, then reduce the heat and cook over a low heat for about 40 minutes, or until the water has completely evaporated. Increase the heat a little and keep cooking for about 20 minutes, stirring regularly, so the peanuts caramelise. Spread them out on a baking tray lined with baking paper and allow them to cool. Roughly chop.

ASSEMBLY

If the Salidou frozen yoghurt was made ahead of time, take it out of the freezer 10 minutes before piping to make it more malleable. Using a spatula, fill the piping bag (nozzle attached) with yoghurt. Pipe out the frozen yoghurt soft-serve style into six small serving dishes, and top with the home-made chouchous. Serve immediately.

FROZEN COCO-MARRONS
CHOCOLATE BASE + MARRONS GLACÉ TOPPING

makes 6 frozen yoghurts
preparation time 10 minutes
cooking time 10 minutes

800 g (1 lb 12 oz) CHOCOLATE
FROZEN YOGHURT ✳
180 g (6 oz) MARRONS GLACÉS (CANDIED
CHESTNUTS) ✳

chocolate sauce
2 TABLESPOONS THIN (POURING) CREAM
200 ml (7 fl oz) MILK
200 g (7 oz) DARK CHOCOLATE
40 g (1½ oz) UNSALTED BUTTER
2 TABLESPOONS CASTER (SUPERFINE) SUGAR

equipment
PIPING (ICING) BAG AND STAR NOZZLE

✳ The recipe for this is on page 26. Marrons glacés are peeled chestnuts that have been candied in a sugar syrup. Look for them in speciality food stores, particularly around Christmas time.

PREPARATION
Place the piping bag and nozzle in the freezer for a few minutes so they are well chilled.

CHOCOLATE SAUCE
Heat the cream and milk over a low heat. Take the saucepan off the heat before the mixture comes to the boil. Add the chocolate, broken into pieces, and stir with a wooden spoon until the chocolate has melted. Return the saucepan to a low heat, add the butter and sugar and heat, stirring, until the mixture is smooth.

ASSEMBLY
If the frozen yoghurt is in the freezer, take it out 10 minutes ahead of time. Using a spatula, fill the piping bag (nozzle attached) with yoghurt. Pipe out the yoghurt soft-serve style into six small serving dishes, scatter over the marrons glacés and pour over the chocolate sauce. Serve immediately.

MARCEL'S EXTRAS

Chocolate sauce will keep for up to 2 weeks in a sealed jar in the refrigerator. Soften over a bowl of hot water to pouring consistency.

frozen yoghurts

FROZEN SALIDOU AND CHURROS

SALTED BUTTER CARAMEL BASE + CHURROS TOPPING

makes 6 frozen yoghurts
preparation time 20 minutes
cooking time 15 minutes

800 g (1 lb 12 oz) SALIDOU FROZEN YOGHURT ✳

chocolate sauce
2 TABLESPOONS THIN (POURING) CREAM
200 ml (7 fl oz) MILK
200 g (7 oz) DARK CHOCOLATE
40 g (1½ oz) UNSALTED BUTTER
2 TABLESPOONS CASTER (SUPERFINE) SUGAR

churros
NEUTRAL OIL, FOR DEEP-FRYING
300 ml (10½ fl oz) WATER
200 g (7 oz/1⅓ cups) PLAIN (ALL-PURPOSE) FLOUR
2 TEASPOONS SUGAR
60 g (2¼ oz/½ cup) ICING (CONFECTIONERS') SUGAR

equipment
PIPING (ICING) BAG AND STAR NOZZLE

✳ The recipe for this is on page 26. Salidou is a French brand of salted butter caramel spread. Use a good-quality equivalent from a speciality food store or delicatessen if you can't track it down.

PREPARATION

Place the piping bag and nozzle in the freezer for a few minutes so they are well chilled.

CHOCOLATE SAUCE

Heat the cream and milk over a low heat. Take the saucepan off the heat before the mixture comes to the boil. Add the chocolate, broken into pieces, and stir with a wooden spoon until the chocolate has melted. Return the saucepan to the low heat, add the butter and sugar, and heat, stirring, until the mixture is smooth.

CHURROS

Fill a large saucepan about a third full with the oil and heat it over a medium heat until very hot. Bring the water to the boil in a separate saucepan. Work the flour, sugar and boiling water together with a spatula until you have a smooth dough. Shape the dough with your hands into small sausages about 1 cm (½ inch) thick and 5 cm (2 inches) long. If you want fluted churros (like the ones in the picture), you can put the mixture into a piping back with a star nozzle and pipe them into little sausages. Carefully drop the dough sausages into the bubbling oil and cook for 2 minutes, then drain on paper towels. Sprinkle them with the icing sugar then cut them into 1 cm sections.

ASSEMBLY

If the frozen yoghurt is in the freezer, take it out 10 minutes ahead of time. Using a spatula, fill the piping bag (nozzle attached) with yoghurt. Pipe out the yoghurt soft-serve style into six small serving bowls, scatter over the pieces of churros and pour over the chocolate sauce. Serve immediately.

MARCEL'S EXTRAS

Chocolate sauce will keep for up to 2 weeks in a sealed jar in the refrigerator. Soften over a bowl of hot water to pouring consistency.

frozen yoghurts

HONEY–NUT FROZEN YOGHURT

makes 6 frozen yoghurts
preparation time 10 minutes
churning time 25 to 30 minutes

honey–nut frozen yoghurt
750 g (1 lb 10 oz) GREEK YOGHURT
3 TABLESPOONS HONEY
2 TEASPOONS VANILLA SUGAR
120 g (4¼ oz/1 cup) CHOPPED WALNUTS

assembly
HONEY
WALNUTS

equipment
ICE-CREAM MAKER

METHOD
The night before, place the bowl of the ice-cream maker in the freezer. Whisk the yoghurt with the honey and vanilla sugar. Pour this mixture into the ice-cream maker and churn for 25–30 minutes. Add the walnuts and churn for another 2–3 minutes.

ASSEMBLY
If the frozen yoghurt was made ahead of time, take it out of the freezer 10 minutes before to make it more malleable. Scoop balls of frozen yoghurt and drizzle with honey and extra walnuts.

MARCEL'S TIP
At serving time, add raisins, dried apricots or dried figs.

frozen yoghurts

GREEN TEA FROZEN YOGHURT
AND ROLLED WAFER BISCUITS

makes 6 frozen yoghurts
preparation time 10 minutes
cooking time 5 minutes
cooling time 1 hour
churning time 25 minutes

tea-infused yoghurt
500 g (1 lb 2 oz) FAT-FREE YOGHURT
150 ml (5 fl oz) LOW-FAT MILK
30 g (1 oz) GREEN TEA LEAVES
(IMPERIAL° KUSMI TEA, IF POSSIBLE) ✳

green tea frozen yoghurt
500 g (1 lb 2 oz) TEA-INFUSED YOGHURT
(SEE ABOVE)
75 g (2½ oz/⅓ cup) SUGAR
200 ml (7 fl oz) THIN (POURING) CREAM
12 ROLLED WAFER BISCUITS (COOKIES)

equipment
ICE-CREAM MAKER, ELECTRIC BEATER,
PIPING (ICING) BAG AND STAR NOZZLE

✳ *This is our preferred blend, but you can use any green or sencha leaf tea instead of the Kusmi.*

TEA-INFUSED YOGHURT
Heat the milk in a saucepan, then remove from the heat before it reaches boiling point. Add the tea leaves to the hot milk, stir gently, cover and leave to infuse for 3 minutes. Strain the milk, transfer it to an airtight container and store in the refrigerator for 1 hour until the mixture is quite cold. Add 30 ml (1 fl oz) of the infused milk to the fat-free yoghurt and whisk until the mixture is smooth.

GREEN TEA FROZEN YOGHURT
Whisk the yoghurt and sugar together. Beat the cream in a separate bowl with the electric beater to thicken it, then add the yoghurt and sugar mixture. Whisk together. Pour the mixture into an ice-cream maker and churn for about 25 minutes.

ASSEMBLY
Place the piping bag and nozzle in the freezer for a few minutes so they are well chilled. If the green tea frozen yoghurt is in the freezer, take it out 10 minutes ahead of time. Using a spatula, fill the piping bag (nozzle attached) with yoghurt. Pipe out the yoghurt soft-serve style into six small serving bowls. Cut the rolled wafer biscuits in half. Stick one half in each serving of yoghurt, and crumble the remaining halves over the top.

MARCEL'S EXTRAS

The leftover infused milk can be used in a recipe for madeleines or a cake instead of regular milk. It will keep for 2–3 days in the refrigerator, but can also be frozen.

CHEESECAKE FROZEN YOGHURT

makes 6 frozen yoghurts
preparation time 20 minutes
churning time 20 to 25 minutes

10 DIGESTIVE-STYLE BISCUITS (COOKIES)
170 g (6 oz) CREAM CHEESE
250 g (9 oz) GREEK YOGHURT
180 g (6 oz) RAW (DEMERARA) SUGAR
2 TABLESPOONS LEMON JUICE
2 TEASPOONS VANILLA BEAN PASTE
300 g (10½ oz) BERRIES OF YOUR CHOICE

equipment
ICE-CREAM MAKER
PIPING (ICING) BAG AND STAR NOZZLE

METHOD

The night before, place the bowl of the ice-cream maker in the freezer. Finely crush four of the biscuits. Work the cream cheese with a fork to soften. Beat the yoghurt, cream cheese, crushed biscuits, sugar, lemon juice and vanilla bean paste until smooth and airy. Transfer to the bowl of the ice-cream maker and churn for 20–25 minutes, depending on the consistency you prefer. Meanwhile, wash the berries and cut them into pieces, and crumble the remaining biscuits.

ASSEMBLY

Place the piping bag and nozzle in the freezer for a few minutes so they are well chilled. If the frozen yoghurt is in the freezer, take it out 10 minutes ahead of time. Using a spatula, fill the piping bag (nozzle attached) with yoghurt. Pipe out the frozen yoghurt soft-serve style into six small serving bowls, then top with the crumbled biscuits and berries. Serve immediately.

COOKIE DOUGH FROZEN YOGHURT
WITH DULCE DE LECHE

makes 6 frozen yoghurts
preparation time 20 minutes
churning time 5 minutes
cooking time 1 hour
cooling time 15 minutes

800 g (1 lb 12 oz) NATURAL FROZEN YOGHURT ✳

cookie dough
125 g (4½ oz) LIGHTLY SALTED BUTTER, SOFTENED
55 g (2 oz/¼ cup) SUGAR
45 g (1¾ oz/¼ cup) LIGHT BROWN SUGAR
1 EGG
185 g (6½ oz/1¼ cups) PLAIN (ALL-PURPOSE) FLOUR
1 TEASPOON BAKING POWDER
1 PINCH FINE SEA SALT
60 g (2¼ oz/⅓ cup) CHOCOLATE CHIPS

dulce de leche
1 litre (35 fl oz/4 cups) MILK
350 g (12 oz) CASTER (SUPERFINE) SUGAR
1 TEASPOON BICARBONATE OF
SODA (BAKING SODA)
1 VANILLA BEAN
1 PINCH FINE SEA SALT

equipment
ICE-CREAM MAKER
ELECTRIC BEATER

COOKIE DOUGH
Beat the butter and sugars together in a bowl with an electric beater until pale and creamy. Add the egg, then the sifted flour, baking powder and salt. Combine until the mixture is smooth. Add the chocolate chips and stir through. Form the dough into small teaspoon-sized balls.

COOKIE DOUGH FROZEN YOGHURT
Add the balls of cookie dough to the natural frozen yoghurt, transfer to the ice-cream maker and churn for 5 minutes.

DULCE DE LECHE
Put all of the ingredients into a saucepan and heat over a high heat, stirring constantly. When the milk begins to colour, reduce the heat to medium and let the mixture thicken, continuing to stir until you have a sauce-like consistency. Stop the cooking process by dipping the base of the saucepan in a large container of cold water. Remove the vanilla bean.

ASSEMBLY
If the frozen yoghurt is in the freezer, take it out 10 minutes ahead of time. Scoop out balls of frozen yoghurt into six serving bowls and top with dulce de leche.

✳ *The recipe for this is on page 24.*

✳ *The recipe for this is on page 24.*

MARCEL'S EXTRAS

The leftover dulce de leche can be stored in an airtight container in the refrigerator for up to 2 weeks.

frozen yoghurts

SHEEP'S MILK FROZEN YOGHURT
WITH BASIL COULIS + TOASTED HAZELNUTS

makes 6 frozen yoghurts
preparation time 15 minutes
churning time 25 to 30 minutes

sheep's milk frozen yoghurt

500 g (1 lb 2 oz) SHEEP'S MILK YOGHURT
1 TABLESPOON LEMON JUICE
250 ml (9 fl oz/1 cup) THICKENED
(WHIPPING) CREAM
1 PINCH FINE SEA SALT
115 g (4 oz/¾ cup) TOASTED HAZELNUTS,
ROUGHLY CHOPPED

basil coulis

ABOUT 10–12 BASIL LEAVES
120 ml (4 fl oz) OLIVE OIL
1 GARLIC CLOVE
SALT AND PEPPER

equipment

ICE-CREAM MAKER
ELECTRIC BEATER
PIPING (ICING) BAG AND STAR NOZZLE

PREPARATION

The night before, place the bowl of the ice-cream maker in
the freezer.

SHEEP'S MILK FROZEN YOGHURT

Place the beater attachments and bowl for whipping the cream in
the freezer. Whisk the yoghurt with the lemon juice in a bowl.
Whip the cream and salt in a separate bowl and fold it gently into
the first mixture. Churn this mixture in the ice-cream maker for
25–30 minutes.

BASIL COULIS

Meanwhile, chop the basil leaves (reserve a few for garnishing) with
the olive oil and garlic. Season with salt and pepper and pass through
a fine sieve.

ASSEMBLY

Place the piping bag and nozzle in the freezer for a few minutes so
they are well chilled. If the frozen yoghurt is in the freezer, take it
out 10 minutes ahead of time. Using a spatula, fill the piping bag
(nozzle attached) with yoghurt. Pipe out the frozen yoghurt
soft-serve style into six small serving dishes, drizzle with the basil
coulis, scatter over some chopped hazelnuts and serve immediately.

frozen yoghurts

MANGO–LIME FROZEN YOGHURT
INSTANT FROZEN YOGHURT

makes 6 frozen yoghurts
preparation time 10 minutes
freezing time 45 minutes + 1 hour (optional)

375 g (13 oz) GREEK YOGHURT
1 LARGE LIME
600 g (1 lb 5 oz) FROZEN MANGO, CUT INTO CUBES
3–4 TEASPOONS RAW (DEMERARA) SUGAR

equipment
BLENDER

METHOD
For a good frozen consistency, put the yoghurt in the freezer for 45 minutes before starting the recipe. Finely grate the lime zest and set aside in the refrigerator. Squeeze the lime. Place the cubes of mango, the yoghurt, sugar and lime juice in the blender. Blend until you have a mixture that's almost smooth, being careful not to over-blend so you don't lose the frozen consistency.

ASSEMBLY
For a firmer consistency, transfer the frozen yoghurt to a suitable container and place in the freezer for 1 hour. Scoop into balls, sprinkle with the grated lime zest and serve immediately.

MARCEL'S EXTRA IDEA

Sprinkle your frozen yoghurts with coconut shavings or desiccated coconut.

FROZEN SOY YOGHURT
INSTANT FROZEN YOGHURT

makes 6 frozen yoghurts
preparation time 10 minutes
freezing time 4 hours (unless the fruit is already frozen) + 45 minutes
+ 1 hour (optional)

750 g (1 lb 10 oz) SOY MILK YOGHURT
2 WELL-RIPENED BANANAS
300 g (10½ oz) BLACKBERRIES
300 ml (10½ fl oz) SOY CREAM
3 TABLESPOONS RAW (DEMERARA) SUGAR

equipment
BLENDER

METHOD

Slice the bananas into thick rounds and put them in the freezer with the blackberries for about 4 hours. For a good frozen consistency, put the yoghurt in the freezer for 45 minutes. Process the frozen bananas and blackberries, the yoghurt, soy cream and sugar in the blender, until the mixture is almost smooth, being careful not to over-blend so you don't lose the frozen consistency.

ASSEMBLY

For a firmer consistency, transfer the frozen yoghurt to a suitable container and place in the freezer for 1 hour. Scoop into balls and serve immediately.

MARCEL'S EXTRAS

Soy cream can be found in health food stores and speciality food stores. If you can't find soy cream, you can use soy milk instead.

frozen yoghurts

RASPBERRY–PECAN FROZEN YOGHURT
INSTANT FROZEN YOGHURT

makes 6 frozen yoghurts
preparation time 10 minutes
freezing time 45 minutes + 1 hour (optional)

150 g (5½ oz) MASCARPONE CHEESE
375 g (13 oz) GREEK YOGHURT
350 g (12 oz) FROZEN RASPBERRIES
2 TEASPOONS RAW (DEMERARA) SUGAR
6 TABLESPOONS CHOPPED PECANS
12 CHOCOLATE BISCUITS (COOKIES)

equipment
BLENDER
PIPING (ICING) BAG AND STAR NOZZLE

METHOD

For a good frozen consistency, put the mascarpone cheese in the freezer for 45 minutes. Put the yoghurt, frozen raspberries, mascarpone and sugar in the blender and blend until you have a mixture that's almost smooth, being careful not to over-blend so you don't lose the frozen consistency.

ASSEMBLY

For a firmer consistency, transfer the frozen yoghurt to a suitable container and place in the freezer for 1 hour. Place the piping bag and nozzle in the freezer for a few minutes so they are well chilled. Using a spatula, fill the piping bag (nozzle attached) with frozen yoghurt. Pipe out the frozen yoghurt soft-serve style into six small serving dishes, then top with the pecans and crumbled chocolate biscuits. Serve immediately.

MARCEL'S EXTRA INDULGENCE

Caramelise the pecans: preheat the oven to 180°C (350°F/Gas 4); put the pecans, 1 tablespoon honey and 1 teaspoon sugar in a bowl; mix with a spoon to coat the nuts, then spread on a baking tray lined with baking paper and bake for 10 minutes. Allow to cool before scattering over the frozen yoghurts.

FROZEN BIRCHER
INSTANT FROZEN YOGHURT

makes 6 frozen yoghurts
preparation time 10 minutes
freezing time 4 hours (unless the fruit is already frozen) + 45 minutes
+ 1 hour (optional)

375 g (13 oz) GREEK YOGHURT
5 BANANAS (4 WELL-RIPENED AND 1 LESS RIPE)
115 g (4 oz/¾ cup) SKINNED HAZELNUTS
1½ TABLESPOONS STORE-BOUGHT MUESLI
(GRANOLA)
3 TABLESPOONS HONEY, PLUS
EXTRA TO DRIZZLE (OPTIONAL)

equipment
BLENDER

METHOD
Slice the well-ripened bananas into thick rounds, put them in a freezer-safe container and freeze for about 4 hours. For a good frozen consistency, put the yoghurt in the freezer for 45 minutes. Roughly chop the hazelnuts. Slice the less-ripe banana into rounds, put it in a bowl, add the muesli and mix. Put the frozen banana, yoghurt and honey into the blender jug and blend until you have a mixture that's almost smooth, being careful not to over-blend so you don't lose the frozen consistency.

ASSEMBLY
For a firmer consistency, transfer the frozen yoghurt to a suitable container and place in the freezer for 1 hour. Scoop into balls and sprinkle with the banana muesli. Add a drizzle of honey according to taste. Serve immediately.

HONEY–CHERRY FROZEN YOGHURT
INSTANT FROZEN YOGHURT

makes 6 frozen yoghurts
preparation time 10 minutes
freezing time 4 hours (unless the fruit is already frozen)
+ 1 hour (optional)

750 g (1 lb 10 oz) GREEK YOGHURT
600 g (1 lb 5 oz) CHERRIES, PITTED
12 FRESH DATES
6 TABLESPOONS HONEY

equipment
BLENDER
PIPING (ICING) BAG AND STAR NOZZLE

METHOD

Place the yoghurt and cherries separately in suitable containers and place them in the freezer for about 4 hours. Pit the dates and cut them into small pieces. Put the frozen yoghurt and cherries in the blender. Add the honey and process until the lumps are gone, being careful not to over-blend so you don't lose the frozen consistency.

ASSEMBLY

For a firmer consistency, transfer the frozen yoghurt to a suitable container and place in the freezer for 1 hour. Place the piping bag and nozzle in the freezer for a few minutes so they are well chilled. Using a spatula, fill the piping bag (nozzle attached) with frozen yoghurt. Pipe out the frozen yoghurt soft-serve style into six small serving dishes, top with the date pieces and serve immediately.

WHITE CHOC–BLACKCURRANT FROZEN YOGHURT

INSTANT FROZEN YOGHURT

makes 6 frozen yoghurts
preparation time 10 minutes
freezing time 45 minutes + 1 hour (optional)

375 g (13 oz) GREEK YOGHURT
180 g (6 oz) WHITE CHOCOLATE
600 g (1 lb 5 oz) FROZEN BLACKCURRANTS
3–4 TEASPOONS RAW (DEMERARA) SUGAR,
TO TASTE

equipment
BLENDER

METHOD

For a good frozen consistency, put the yoghurt in the freezer for 45 minutes before starting the recipe. Make shavings of white chocolate with a vegetable peeler, and set aside in the refrigerator. Place all the other ingredients in a blender and blend until you have a mixture that's almost smooth, being careful not to over-blend so you don't lose the frozen consistency.

ASSEMBLY

For a firmer consistency, transfer the frozen yoghurt to a suitable container and place in the freezer for 1 hour. Scoop into balls, sprinkle with the shavings of white chocolate and serve immediately.

frozen yoghurt sandwiches

FROZEN SHORTBREADS

makes 6 frozen yoghurt shortbread sandwiches
preparation time 30 minutes
cooking time 10 to 12 minutes
refrigeration time 1 hour + 20 minutes
cooling time 15 minutes

12 large shortbread biscuits
250 g (9 oz/1⅔ cups) PLAIN (ALL-PURPOSE) FLOUR
1 TEASPOON BAKING POWDER
½ TEASPOON SALT
1 VANILLA BEAN, SEEDS SCRAPED
180 g (6 oz) UNSALTED BUTTER
165 g (5¾ oz/¾ cup) SUGAR
4 SMALL EGG YOLKS

filling
400 g (14 oz) NATURAL FROZEN YOGHURT ✳
6 LARGE STRAWBERRIES

equipment
12 x 8 cm (3¼ inch) PASTRY RINGS

✳ *The recipe for this is on page 24.*

SHORTBREAD BISCUITS

Work the flour, baking powder, salt, vanilla seeds and butter, cut into small pieces, together with your hands until you have a coarse sandy texture. Add the sugar and rub it through. Make a well in the dough, put the egg yolks in it, cover them with dough mixture and crush them with the palm of your hand. Cover with mixture again and repeat until the egg yolks are completely incorporated (take care not to overwork the dough). Lightly flatten the ball of dough, cover with plastic wrap and set aside for 1 hour in the refrigerator. Preheat the oven to 170°C (325°F/Gas 3). Flour your work surface and rolling pin and roll out the dough to a thickness of 1 cm (½ inch). Cut 12 circles using the pastry rings and place each biscuit, still inside its ring, on a baking tray lined with baking paper. Refrigerate for 20 minutes to firm the dough. Bake in the oven for 10–12 minutes. When the biscuits are baked and nicely browned, let them cool for 15 minutes before removing the rings.

ASSEMBLY

Wash the strawberries, hull them and cut them into rounds. Spread six shortbreads with a large scoop of frozen yoghurt, then top with the sliced strawberries. Place a thin layer of frozen yoghurt on top, cover with a second shortbread and press down to spread the frozen yoghurt over the whole surface. Smooth the sides of the sandwiches with a knife to trim any overflow.

MARCEL'S TIPS: WHAT VARIATIONS CAN I MAKE TO THIS RECIPE?

You can replace the strawberries with kiwi fruit, mango, pineapple or cherries, depending on the season … You can also use flavoured frozen yoghurt, or any other sorbet or ice cream (salted butter caramel, chocolate, berry …).

FROZEN WAFFLES

makes 6 frozen yoghurt waffles
preparation time 30 minutes
cooking time 4 to 5 minutes each
resting time 2 hours 40 minutes

6 Belgian waffles

10 g (3 TEASPOONS) DRIED YEAST
100 ml (3½ fl oz) LUKEWARM MILK
225 g (8 oz/1½ cups) PLAIN (ALL-PURPOSE) FLOUR,
PLUS 75 g (2½ oz/½ CUP) EXTRA TO KNEAD IN
1 PINCH SALT
2 TABLESPOONS RAW (DEMERARA) SUGAR
1 EGG, LIGHTLY BEATEN
140 g (5 oz) UNSALTED BUTTER, SOFTENED
100 g (3½ oz) PEARL (NIB) SUGAR

filling

400 g (14 oz) CHOCOLATE FROZEN YOGHURT ✳
170 g (6 oz) BERRIES (RASPBERRIES OR
REDCURRANTS, FOR THEIR ACIDITY)

equipment

WAFFLE IRON

METHOD

Dissolve the yeast in the warm milk. Sift 225 g of flour and the salt into a large bowl and add the sugar. Make a well in the centre and pour in the egg and the yeast mixture, then leave for 10 minutes. Mix together, using your hands to form a rough ball and rest for 15 minutes. Knead the dough for about 5 minutes until it is elastic. Spread out the dough on a floured work surface and gradually incorporate the butter using your hands (it will be very sticky). Add the extra flour gradually to form a smooth ball of elastic dough. Cover with plastic wrap and let the dough rise at room temperature for at least 2 hours until doubled in volume. Add the pearl sugar, mix in and separate the dough into balls, about 100 g (3½ oz) each. Let them rest for another 15 minutes. Heat the waffle iron, place a ball of dough in the middle of the plate and cook for 4–5 minutes, or until the waffle is golden brown. Repeat with the remaining dough portions.

ASSEMBLY

Place a scoop of chocolate frozen yoghurt on each hot waffle and scatter over the berries. Serve immediately.

✳ *The recipe for this is on page 26.*

MARCEL'S TIPS

Pearl sugar (also called nib or hail sugar) is coarse white sugar available from speciality food stores. You can replace the chocolate frozen yoghurt with a sorbet (such as gooseberry or blueberry) or a bitter cocoa ice cream. The filling shouldn't be too sweet, as Belgian waffles are already very sweet.

FROZEN PEANUT BUTTER COOKIES

makes 6 frozen yoghurt cookie sandwiches
preparation time 20 minutes
cooking time 10 to 12 minutes
refrigeration time 20 minutes

12 cookies (biscuits)

40 g (1½ oz) UNSALTED BUTTER, SOFTENED
90 g (3¼ oz/⅓ cup) PEANUT BUTTER
2 TABLESPOONS SUGAR
2 TABLESPOONS RAW (DEMERARA) SUGAR
½ VANILLA BEAN, SEEDS SCRAPED
1 SMALL EGG
50 g (1¾ oz/⅓ cup) PLAIN (ALL-PURPOSE) FLOUR
1 SMALL PINCH SALT
½ TEASPOON BAKING POWDER

filling

400 g (14 oz) VANILLA FROZEN YOGHURT ✳

METHOD

Preheat the oven to 165°C (320°F/Gas 3). Whisk together the butter, peanut butter, sugars and vanilla seeds. Add the egg and mix again. Sift the flour, salt and baking powder over the bowl and mix until smooth. Refrigerate for 20 minutes to firm. Line a baking tray with baking paper. Using floured hands, divide the dough into 12 small balls and arrange them on the tray, spacing them out from each other and evenly flatten a little. Bake for about 10–12 minutes: the edge of each cookie should be golden brown and the middle risen. Take the cookies out of the oven and wait until they are cool enough to handle.

ASSEMBLY

Top six cookies with a large scoop of vanilla frozen yoghurt, top the sandwiches with a second cookie and press down firmly with your palm to flatten the frozen yoghurt in the middle. Serve immediately.

✳ *The recipe for this is on page 26.*

FROZEN BROWNIES

makes 6 frozen yoghurt brownie sandwiches
preparation time 20 minutes
cooking time 25 minutes
cooling time 1 hour

12 brownies

100 g (3½ oz/1 cup) PECANS
55 g (2 oz) LIGHTLY SALTED BUTTER
150 g (5½ oz) DARK CHOCOLATE
110 g (3¾ oz/½ cup) SUGAR
1 SMALL EGG
75 g (2½ oz/1½ cups) PLAIN (ALL-PURPOSE) FLOUR

filling

400 g (14 oz) VANILLA FROZEN YOGHURT ✳

equipment

16 cm (6¼ inch) SQUARE CAKE TIN

✳ *The recipe for this is on page 26.*

METHOD

Preheat the oven to 180°C (350°F/Gas 4). Roast the pecans: spread them out on a baking tray lined with baking paper and place in the oven for 10 minutes. Chop them with a knife and set aside 30 g (1 oz/¼ cup) for later. Melt the butter and chocolate in a double boiler. Remove from the heat, add the sugar to the hot butter and chocolate and mix. Stir in the egg, then add the sifted flour and beat vigorously for at least 1 minute. Add the pecans and mix. Grease the cake tin and line the base with baking paper. Pour in the brownie batter and bake for 15 minutes, or until the brownie is firm. Let it cool in the refrigerator for 1 hour, then turn out and cut into 12 pieces.

ASSEMBLY

Spread a layer of vanilla frozen yoghurt on six brownies, sprinkle with the reserved pecans and add a second layer of frozen yoghurt. Top with the six remaining brownies and serve immediately.

FROZEN SPECULAAS

makes 6 frozen yoghurt speculaas sandwiches
preparation time 15 minutes
cooling time 1 hour

400 g (14 oz) STRAWBERRY FROZEN YOGHURT ✳
150 g (5½ oz) DARK CHOCOLATE, CHOPPED
125 ml (4 fl oz/½ cup) MILK
18 SPECULAAS BISCUITS (COOKIES)

✳ *The recipe for this is on page 26.*

METHOD

Melt the chocolate in a double boiler with the milk. Dip nine speculaas biscuits in the melted chocolate, one by one, and let them set for 1 hour in the refrigerator on a wire rack. There may seem to be a huge amount of melted chocolate, but that's what it takes to coat the biscuits perfectly.

ASSEMBLY

Place a large spoonful of strawberry frozen yoghurt on a plain speculaas. Top with a chocolate speculaas and press gently with the palm of your hand to spread the yoghurt across the whole surface without breaking the biscuits. Smooth the sides with a knife to trim any overflow. Repeat the process to make a second storey, with a new layer of frozen yoghurt and a plain speculaas on top. Make six sandwiches in this way, alternating sandwiches with two chocolate speculaas and one plain, and sandwiches with two plain speculaas and one chocolate. Serve immediately.

MARCEL'S STYLE TIPS

To make the chocolate on the biscuits glossy, melt it in a double boiler in a container that doesn't touch the water. When it's melted by being 'steamed', the chocolate becomes even shinier.

yoghurt

combos

PRALINE YOGHURT
AND STRAWBERRIES

makes 4 yoghurts
preparation time 15 minutes
cooking time 15 minutes

500 g (1 lb 2 oz) STIRRED OR GREEK YOGHURT
100 g (3½ oz) STRAWBERRIES, HULLED

home-made praline
50 g (1¾ oz/⅓ cup) BLANCHED HAZELNUTS
55 g (2 oz/⅓ cup) BLANCHED ALMONDS
110 g (3¾ oz/½ cup) SUGAR

equipment
FOOD PROCESSOR

METHOD
Toast the hazelnuts and almonds for a few minutes in a dry frying pan. Remove to a lightly greased baking tray. Add the sugar and 1 tablespoon water to the frying pan. Stir over a low heat to melt the sugar, brushing the sides with a wet pastry brush. Increase the heat and let it caramelise, without stirring. Pour over the nuts and let it cool. Once cooled, grind the praline in the food processor. Wash the strawberries and dice them.

ASSEMBLY
Divide the yoghurt between four serving bowls, then add the strawberries and sprinkle over the praline. Stir and serve immediately.

MARCEL'S EASY SHORTCUT

The home-made praline can easily be replaced by a store-bought version.

GREEN TEA YOGHURT
AND EXOTIC FRUIT

makes 4 yoghurts
preparation time 10 minutes
cooling time 1 hour

infused yoghurt
500 g (1 lb 2 oz) STIRRED FAT-FREE YOGHURT
150 ml (5 fl oz) SKIM MILK
20 g (¾ oz/¼ cup) GREEN TEA LEAVES
(DETOX° KUSMI TEA, IF POSSIBLE)

topping
½ PINEAPPLE
2 KIWI FRUIT
125 g (4½ oz) STRAWBERRIES, HULLED
4 TABLESPOONS BLANCHED ALMONDS

METHOD
Heat the milk in a saucepan and remove from the heat before it reaches boiling point. Add the tea, stir and cover. Let it infuse for 3 minutes. Strain the infused milk through a fine sieve. Pour into a container with a lid, seal and set aside in the refrigerator for 1 hour. Peel the pineapple and cut it into small cubes. Peel the kiwi fruit and dice. Cut the strawberries into chunks. Pour 3 teaspoons of the tea-infused milk into the yoghurt and mix well.

ASSEMBLY
Arrange the pieces of kiwi fruit and pineapple in the bottom of four serving glasses. Cover them with yoghurt and top with the strawberries and almonds. Serve immediately.

MARCEL'S TIPS

The leftover infused milk can be used in a recipe for madeleines or a cake instead of regular milk. It will keep for 2–3 days in the refrigerator, but can also be frozen.

FRAISE TAGADA YOGHURT
STRAWBERRY JELLY YOGHURT

makes 4 yoghurts
preparation time 10 minutes
cooling time 2 hours 15 minutes
setting time 6 to 8 hours

60 g (2¼ oz) POT-SET FULL-CREAM
NATURAL YOGHURT
8 (ABOUT 40 g/1½ oz) FRAISE TAGADA ✳
(STRAWBERRY JELLY SWEETS)
80 ml (2½ fl oz/⅓ cup) THIN (POURING) CREAM
500 ml (17 fl oz/2 cups) MILK

equipment
YOGHURT MAKER

METHOD

Melt the strawberry jelly sweets in a saucepan with the cream over low heat. Cool the preparation in the refrigerator, then add the yoghurt and whisk until the mixture is smooth. Stir in the milk, whisking again. Pour the mixture into the pots of the yoghurt maker and let them set; allow between 6 and 8 hours, depending on the manufacturer's instructions. Refrigerate for another 2 hours and crumble over a little biscuit (cookie) right before serving, if you like.

✳ *Fraise Tagada is a French brand of jelly sweets. They are pink strawberry-flavoured candies covered in fine sugar. You can find them in some speciality stores and delicatessens. You can also substitute them with any strawberry jelly sweets.*

BIRCHER YOGHURT
WITH GRATED APPLE + HAZELNUTS

makes 4 large yoghurts
preparation time 10 minutes
soaking time 1 hour
cooking time 10 minutes

250 g (9 oz) STIRRED YOGHURT
75 g (2½ oz/¾ cup) BABY (QUICK) OAT FLAKES
185 ml (6 fl oz/¾ cup) LUKEWARM WATER
4 PINCHES GROUND CINNAMON (OPTIONAL)
50 g (1¾ oz/⅓ cup) SKINNED HAZELNUTS
80 ml (2½ fl oz/⅓ cup) AGAVE SYRUP
4 TART APPLES (GRANNY SMITH,
ARIANE ...), PEELED, CORED AND GRATED

METHOD
Preheat the oven to 180°C (350°F/Gas 4). Soak the oats for 1 hour in the lukewarm water, sprinkled with cinnamon, if using. To roast the hazelnuts, chop them roughly, spread them out on a baking tray lined with baking paper and place in the oven for 10 minutes. Stir the oats with a fork, add the yoghurt, agave syrup, grated apples and roasted hazelnuts. Stir, divide among four serving bowls and serve immediately.

MARCEL'S CULTURE FLASH: WHAT IS BIRCHER?

Behind this cult dish, an icon of the vegetarian and hippie movement, lies the health secret of a mountain shepherd: crushed wheat in milk with honey and small pieces of apple. At the beginning of the twentieth century, Zurich's Dr. Bircher-Benner discovered this recipe and recommended it to his dieting patients!

yoghurt combos

MAPLE SYRUP YOGHURT
AND CARAMELISED PECANS

makes 4 yoghurts
preparation time 10 minutes
cooking time 10 minutes
cooling time 10 minutes

500 g (1 lb 2 oz) STIRRED OR GREEK YOGHURT
50 g (1¾ oz/½ cup) PECANS
1 TABLESPOON SUGAR
25 ml (¾ fl oz) MAPLE SYRUP

METHOD

Preheat the oven to 180°C (350°F/Gas 4). Roughly chop the pecans and mix them in a bowl with the sugar and 1 teaspoon of the maple syrup. Spread this mixture over a baking tray lined with baking paper and bake for about 10 minutes. Remove from the oven and allow to cool.

ASSEMBLY

Divide the yoghurt between four serving bowls, add 1 teaspoon of maple syrup to each and mix. Scatter over the caramelised pecans and serve immediately.

CRÈME DE MARRON YOGHURT
AND MADELEINES

makes 4 yoghurts
preparation time 10 minutes
cooking time 6 to 7 minutes
cooling time 10 minutes

500 g (1 lb 2 oz) STIRRED OR GREEK YOGHURT
4 HEAPED TABLESPOONS OF CRÈME DE MARRONS
(SWEETENED CHESTNUT PURÉE, SMOOTH OR
WITH PIECES)

madeleines
1 EGG
55 g (2 oz/¼ cup) SUGAR
50 g (1¾ oz/⅓ cup) PLAIN (ALL-PURPOSE) FLOUR
60 g (2¼ oz) LIGHTLY SALTED BUTTER, MELTED

equipment
ELECTRIC BEATER
MINI MADELEINE MOULD

METHOD

Preheat the oven to 190°C (375°F/Gas 5). Whisk the egg and sugar together until the mixture doubles in volume. Add the sifted flour and gently mix in with a wooden spoon. Stir in the melted butter (cooled to lukewarm) and mix again. Pour the batter into the buttered madeleine moulds, and bake for 6–7 minutes: the madeleines should be well puffed up and golden around the edge. Allow to cool.

ASSEMBLY

Get four small serving dishes and put a heaped tablespoon of crème de marrons in the bottom of each one. Divide the yoghurt between them and finish with three mini madeleines. Alternatively, stir the crème de marrons through the yoghurt and serve with chopped pieces of madeleines. Serve immediately.

MARCEL, MADELEINE KING

Only fill the mini madeleine moulds three-quarters full so they can rise properly. For even more flavoursome madeleines, make the batter 24 hours before cooking. Store any extra mini madeleines in an airtight container.

MANGO-CHOCOLATE YOGHURT

makes 4 yoghurts
preparation time 15 minutes
refrigeration time 15 minutes

500 g (1 lb 2 oz) STIRRED OR GREEK YOGHURT
1 SMALL MANGO
2 TEASPOONS RAW (DEMERARA) SUGAR
½ VANILLA BEAN, SEEDS SCRAPED
50 g (1¾ oz) DARK CHOCOLATE

equipment
BLENDER

METHOD
Peel the mango, remove the stone, cut the flesh into pieces and process with the sugar and vanilla seeds. Set this sauce aside in the refrigerator until ready to serve. Coarsely grate the dark chocolate.

ASSEMBLY
Divide the yoghurt between four glasses, pour 1 tablespoon of sauce over each serving and add the shavings of chocolate. Serve immediately.

CUCUMBER YOGHURT
SAVOURY RECIPE

makes 4 yoghurts
preparation time 15 minutes
cooking time 10 minutes
cooling time 30 minutes

500 g (1 lb 2 oz) GREEK YOGHURT OR
WHIPPED FROMAGE BLANC
1 LEBANESE (SHORT) CUCUMBER
1 PINCH SALT
1 PINCH PEPPER
DRIZZLE OLIVE OIL

cherry tomato jam
150 g (5½ oz) CHERRY TOMATOES
2 BASIL LEAVES
30 g (1 oz) CASTER (SUPERFINE) SUGAR

METHOD
Wash the cherry tomatoes and basil leaves. Cut the tomatoes in half and shred the basil with scissors. Stew the tomatoes with the sugar over a low heat for 10 minutes, or until syrupy. At the end of the cooking time, add the basil and stir in well. Set aside in the refrigerator until cooled. Peel and finely dice the cucumber. Mix the yoghurt in a bowl with the diced cucumber, salt, pepper and olive oil.

ASSEMBLY
Divide the cucumber yoghurt between four glasses and add 1 heaped tablespoon of tomato jam to each serving.

YOGHURT AND SPECIAL SUGARS

preparation time 2 minutes to 2 weeks (depending on the recipe)

Mix 1 or 2 teaspoons of one of these flavoured sugars into a natural yoghurt. Serve immediately.

LAVENDER SUGAR

makes 1 kg (2 lb 4 oz) sugar • preparation time 2 minutes • resting time 2 weeks

2 TABLESPOONS DRIED LAVENDER,
1 kg (2 lb 4 oz) CASTER (SUPERFINE) SUGAR
equipment STERILE GAUZE

METHOD
Place the lavender in the middle of a piece of sterile gauze and close it up with a rubber band. Place this small bag in a large jar with a lid, cover with sugar and close the jar tightly. Remove the lavender bag when the sugar has absorbed its flavour, after about 2 weeks.

FRAISE TAGADA SUGAR

makes about 400 g (14 oz) sugar • preparation time 3 minutes

25 FRAISE TAGADA (STRAWBERRY JELLY SWEETS) ✳,
400 g (14 oz) CASTER (SUPERFINE) SUGAR
equipment FOOD PROCESSOR

METHOD
Process the strawberry jelly sweets and sugar together to make a homogeneous powder. Store in a sealed jar.

✳ Fraise Tagada is a French brand of jelly sweet. They are pink strawberry-flavoured candies covered in fine sugar. You can find them in some speciality stores and delicatessens. You can also substitute them with any strawberry jelly sweets.

VANILLA SUGAR

makes 1 kg (2 lb 4 oz) sugar • preparation time 1 minute • resting time 1 day

1 kg (2 lb 4 oz) RAW (DEMERARA) SUGAR OR CASTER (SUPERFINE) SUGAR, 2 VANILLA BEANS

METHOD
Pour the caster sugar into a jar. Cut the vanilla beans in half lengthways, bury them in the sugar and seal the jar. Leave it like that for a whole day. Afterwards, leave the pods in the jar, stirring them occasionally, until all the vanilla sugar has been used.

TOFFEE APPLE SUGAR

makes 500 g (1 lb 2 oz) sugar • preparation time 10 minutes • cooling time 15 minutes

500 g (1 lb 2 oz) CASTER (SUPERFINE) SUGAR,
130 ml (4¼ fl oz) THIN (POURING) CREAM,
10 g (¼ oz) UNSALTED BUTTER, 1 PINCH SALT,
50 g (1¾ oz) APPLE CHIPS
equipment FOOD PROCESSOR

METHOD
Pour 400 g (14 oz) of the sugar, the cream, butter and salt into a large saucepan. Place over medium heat and heat, stirring with a spatula, until the butter is melted. Bring the mixture to the boil and cook over a high heat, stirring constantly. When the caramel begins to darken, remove the saucepan from the heat. Pour the caramel onto a large sheet of baking paper and let it cool. Break up the sheet of caramel into pieces about 1 cm (½ inch) square. Process 50 g (1¾ oz) of the toffee pieces with the apple chips to a fine powder, then mix with the remaining sugar. Store in a sealed jar.

milkshakes and lassis

VANILLA MILKSHAKE

makes 1 large glass
preparation time 5 minutes
cooking time 10 minutes
refrigeration time 20 to 30 minutes

200 g (7 oz) NATURAL FROZEN YOGHURT ✳
220 ml (7½ fl oz) LOW-FAT MILK (OR SKIM MILK FOR
A LIGHTER VERSION)
1 VANILLA BEAN, SEEDS SCRAPED
1½ TABLESPOONS AGAVE SYRUP

equipment
BLENDER

✳ *The recipe for this is on page 24.*

METHOD

Pour the milk into a saucepan. Add the vanilla seeds to the milk and heat (without boiling) for about 10 minutes. Strain the milk through a fine sieve and set aside in the refrigerator until well chilled. Put the frozen yoghurt, cold vanilla milk and agave syrup into the blender, and blend: the mixture should be frothy. Pour the mixture into a large glass, add a straw and drink immediately, chilled.

MARCEL'S PRACTICAL SHORTCUTS

You can replace the vanilla bean with ¼ teaspoon vanilla powder that you can put directly into the blender with the milk. You can also replace the vanilla bean and agave syrup with 1 teaspoon of vanilla sugar (see page 106).

milkshakes
and lassis

STRAWBERRY MILKSHAKE

makes 1 large glass
preparation time 5 minutes

200 g (7 oz) NATURAL FROZEN YOGHURT ✳
100 g (3½ oz) STRAWBERRIES, HULLED
220 ml (7½ fl oz) LOW-FAT MILK (OR SKIM MILK FOR
A LIGHTER VERSION)
1 TABLESPOON AGAVE SYRUP

equipment
BLENDER

METHOD
Wash the strawberries and dice them. Put the frozen yoghurt, diced strawberries, milk and agave syrup into the blender and blend until the mixture is frothy. Pour the mixture into a large glass and add a straw. Drink immediately, chilled.

✳ *The recipe for this is on page 24.*

MARCEL'S DIET COACH TIP

If you use skim milk and fat-free frozen yoghurt, the strawberry milkshake is extra, extra light: a true diet ally for guiltless pleasure!

DULCE DE LECHE MILKSHAKE

makes 1 large glass
preparation time 15 minutes
cooking time 20 minutes
cooling time 15 to 20 minutes

200 g (7 oz) NATURAL FROZEN YOGHURT ✳
220 ml (7½ fl oz) LOW-FAT MILK

dulce de leche
250 ml (9 fl oz/1 cup) MILK
75 g (2½ oz/⅓ cup) CASTER (SUPERFINE) SUGAR
¼ TEASPOON BICARBONATE OF SODA
(BAKING SODA)
¼ VANILLA BEAN
1 SMALL PINCH FINE SEA SALT

equipment
BLENDER

✳ *The recipe for this is on page 24.*

METHOD

Put all of the dulce de leche ingredients into a saucepan and heat over a high heat, stirring constantly. When the milk begins to colour, reduce the heat to medium and continue cooking, watching the mixture and stirring until you reach the desired consistency and colour. Remove from the heat and allow to cool in the refrigerator. Remove the vanilla bean. Place the frozen yoghurt, milk and 125 g (4½ oz/½ cup) of the dulce de leche into the blender jug and blend until the mixture is frothy. Pour the mixture into a large glass, add a straw and drink immediately, chilled.

MARCEL'S SPEEDY SHORTCUT

You can save time by buying ready-made dulce de leche from speciality food stores.

BREAKFAST MILKSHAKE

makes 1 large glass
preparation time 5 minutes

200 g (7 oz) NATURAL FROZEN YOGHURT ✳
1 BANANA (ABOUT 100 g/3½ oz)
220 ml (7½ fl oz) SKIM MILK
1 TABLESPOON ROLLED (PORRIDGE) OATS
OR MUESLI FLAKES
3 TEASPOONS AGAVE SYRUP

equipment
BLENDER

✳ *The recipe for this is on page 24.*

METHOD
Slice the banana into rounds. Set one round aside and put the
others in the blender. Add the frozen yoghurt and milk and blend
until the mixture is smooth (approximately 1 minute at maximum
speed). Add the rolled oats and agave syrup and blend for 30 seconds
at a very low speed; the mixture should be frothy. Pour the mixture
into a large glass, press the reserved round of banana onto the edge of
the glass and add a straw. Drink immediately, chilled.

GREEN MILKSHAKE
KIWI FRUIT + SPINACH + SPIRULINA

makes 1 large glass
preparation time 5 minutes

200 g (7 oz) NATURAL FROZEN YOGHURT ✳
1 BANANA (ABOUT 100 g/3½ oz)
1 KIWI FRUIT
220 ml (7½ fl oz) SKIM MILK
1 TEASPOON CHOPPED SPINACH (FRESH OR
FROZEN)
¼ TEASPOON SPIRULINA

equipment
BLENDER

✳ *The recipe for this is on page 24.*

METHOD
Slice the banana into rounds. Peel the kiwi fruit and cut into small triangles. Place the frozen yoghurt, milk, spinach, banana rounds, kiwi fruit triangles and spirulina into the blender and blend until the mixture is frothy. Pour the mixture into a large glass, add a straw and drink immediately, chilled.

MARCEL'S GREEN FLASH

This is the preferred detox beverage of the stars in Los Angeles. It's based on raw leafy green vegetables (40%) and fresh fruit (60%) blended with milk and fresh or frozen yoghurt. You can also use just water or aloe vera juice. Usually no sugar is added, but you can sweeten your drink with agave syrup if you like.

GREEN APPLE MILKSHAKE
GREEN APPLE + KALE

makes 1 large glass
preparation time 5 minutes

200 g (7 oz) NATURAL FROZEN YOGHURT ✳
½ GREEN APPLE (ABOUT 60 g/2¼ oz)
40 g (1½ oz) KALE (STEMS REMOVED)
OR BABY SPINACH
220 ml (7½ fl oz) SKIM MILK
1 TABLESPOON AGAVE SYRUP

equipment
BLENDER

✳ *The recipe for this is on page 24.*

METHOD
Peel and core the apple and cut into small cubes. Wash, dry and shred the kale leaves. Put the frozen yoghurt, milk, diced apple, kale leaves and agave syrup into the blender and blend until the mixture is frothy. Pour the mixture into a large glass, add a straw and drink immediately, chilled.

milkshakes
and lassis

PISTACHIO MILKSHAKE
WITH CHOCOLATE

makes 1 large glass
preparation time 5 minutes

200 g (7 oz) NATURAL OR VANILLA FROZEN
YOGHURT ✳
2 UNSALTED PISTACHIOS, SHELLED
220 ml (7½ fl oz) LOW-FAT MILK
1 TEASPOON PISTACHIO PASTE
1 TEASPOON COCOA POWDER
3 TEASPOONS AGAVE SYRUP

equipment
BLENDER

METHOD
Crush the pistachios into small pieces using a mortar and pestle; set aside. Put the frozen yoghurt, milk, pistachio paste, cocoa powder and agave syrup into the blender and blend until the mixture is frothy. Pour the mixture into a large glass, sprinkle with the crushed pistachio and add a straw. Drink immediately, chilled.

✳ *The recipe for the natural frozen yoghurt is on page 24. The recipe for the vanilla frozen yoghurt is on page 26.*

MARCEL'S COOKING CLASS

For home-made pistachio paste, use equal weights of pistachios and icing sugar. Blanch the pistachios: drop them in boiling water for a few moments, then in cold water. Crush them using a mortar and pestle. Add the icing sugar and, for a smoother paste, add some egg white.

milkshakes and lassis

PRALINE MILKSHAKE
+ CHANTILLY CREAM

makes 1 large glass
preparation time 10 minutes
freezing time 20 minutes

200 g (7 oz) NATURAL OR VANILLA FROZEN
YOGHURT ✳
220 ml (7½ fl oz) LOW-FAT MILK
(OR FULL-CREAM MILK)
1 TABLESPOON PRALINE PASTE

chantilly cream
100 ml (3½ fl oz) THICKENED (WHIPPING) CREAM
1 TABLESPOON ICING (CONFECTIONERS') SUGAR

equipment
BLENDER
ELECTRIC BEATER
PIPING (ICING) BAG AND STAR NOZZLE

CHANTILLY CREAM
Place a mixing bowl and the beater attachments in the freezer for 20 minutes. Pour the cream into the chilled bowl and whip the cream using the electric beater. At the end, add the icing sugar and stir through.

FROZEN YOGHURT
Place the frozen yoghurt, milk and praline paste into the blender and blend until the mixture is frothy.

ASSEMBLY
Pour the mixture into a large glass, pipe a mountain of chantilly cream on top using the piping bag (nozzle attached) and add a straw. Drink immediately, chilled.

✳ The recipe for the natural frozen yoghurt is on page 24. The recipe for the vanilla frozen yoghurt is on page 26.

MARCEL'S TIPS

To make a fake whipped cream using yoghurt, take 100 g (3½ oz) fat-free natural yoghurt, 1 egg white and 20 g (¾ oz) sweetener. Beat the egg white to stiff peaks, then gently fold in the yoghurt with a spatula, taking care not to deflate the egg white. Carefully add the sweetener.
Praline paste is available from speciality food stores. You can also use a hazelnut or almond nut spread.

CHOC–PEAR MILKSHAKE
+ COCOA CHANTILLY CREAM

makes 1 large glass
preparation time 10 minutes
freezer time 20 minutes

200 g (7 oz) NATURAL OR VANILLA FROZEN
YOGHURT ✳
1 SMALL PEAR
220 ml (7½ fl oz) LOW-FAT MILK
(OR FULL-CREAM MILK)
1 TABLESPOON COCOA POWDER, PLUS EXTRA
TO SPRINKLE

cocoa chantilly cream
100 ml (3½ fl oz) THICKENED (WHIPPING) CREAM
1 TABLESPOON ICING (CONFECTIONERS') SUGAR
1 TABLESPOON COCOA POWDER

equipment
BLENDER
ELECTRIC BEATER
PIPING (ICING) BAG AND STAR NOZZLE

COCOA CHANTILLY CREAM
Place a mixing bowl and the beater attachments in the freezer for 20 minutes. Pour the cream into the chilled bowl and whip the cream using the electric beater. At the end, stir in the icing sugar and cocoa powder and stir through.

FROZEN YOGHURT
Peel, core and dice the pear. Place the frozen yoghurt, milk, diced pear and cocoa powder into the blender and blend until the mixture is frothy.

ASSEMBLY
Pour the milkshake mixture into a large glass, pipe a mountain of cocoa chantilly cream on top using the piping bag (nozzle attached) and add a straw. Sprinkle with extra cocoa powder. Drink immediately, chilled.

✳ The recipe for the natural frozen yoghurt is on page 24. The recipe for the vanilla frozen yoghurt is on page 26.

MARCEL'S TIP FOR FLAVOURING YOUR CHANTILLY CREAM

You can add 2 teaspoons of vanilla sugar (see page 106), a few drops of mint, jasmine or other essences, or 2 teaspoons of grated citrus zest to your whipped cream.

SPECULAAS MILKSHAKE

makes 1 large glass
preparation time 5 minutes

200 g (7 oz) NATURAL OR VANILLA FROZEN
YOGHURT ✻
4 SPECULAAS BISCUITS (COOKIES)
220 ml (7½ fl oz) LOW-FAT MILK

equipment
BLENDER

METHOD

Crush one speculaas biscuit and set aside. Roughly chop the others. Place them with the frozen yoghurt and milk in the blender and blend until the mixture is frothy. Pour the mixture into a large glass, sprinkle with the reserved crumbled speculaas and add a straw. Drink immediately, chilled.

✻ The recipe for the natural frozen yoghurt is on page 24. The recipe for the vanilla frozen yoghurt is on page 26.

MARCEL'S DECORATING TIP

Scatter the milkshake with tiny pieces of marshmallow, mini meringues or chocolate shavings.

POMEGRANATE–BANANA LASSI

makes 1 large glass
preparation time 5 minutes

125 g (4½ oz) BULGARIAN YOGHURT ✳
(FAT-FREE OR NORMAL)
½ POMEGRANATE OR
100 ml (3½ fl oz) POMEGRANATE JUICE
½ BANANA
125 ml (4 fl oz/½ cup) LOW-FAT MILK
(OR SKIM MILK FOR A LIGHTER VERSION)
1 TABLESPOON AGAVE SYRUP

equipment
BLENDER

METHOD
Carefully detach the seeds of the pomegranate half. If you want to keep a few seeds whole, for serving, steal a few and drop them into a large serving glass. Slice the half banana into rounds. Put the yoghurt, pomegranate seeds, banana, milk and agave syrup into the blender and blend until the mixture is frothy. Strain through a fine sieve. Pour the mixture into the glass, add a straw and drink immediately, chilled.

✳ *Bulgarian yoghurt is made from sheep's milk and characterised by the unique flavour, which is a result of the sheep grazing in herb-filled pastures. It is starting to become more widely available, but can be substituted with plain yoghurt if you can't find it.*

MARCEL'S GENERAL CULTURE FLASH: THE ORIGIN OF THE LASSI

The lassi is a traditional yoghurt-based drink originally from India. It comes in both sweet and savoury versions, and is an ideal accompaniment to spicy Indian dishes.

MINT-FLEUR DE SEL LASSI

makes 1 large glass
preparation time 5 minutes

125 g (4½ oz) BULGARIAN YOGHURT ✳
(FAT-FREE OR FULL-FAT)
6 MINT LEAVES
1 SMALL PINCH FINE SEA SALT (FLEUR DE SEL)
125 ml (4 fl oz/½ cup) LOW-FAT MILK
(OR SKIM MILK FOR A LIGHTER VERSION)

equipment
BLENDER

METHOD
Wash and dry the mint leaves; set one aside. Place the others in the blender, add the yoghurt, sea salt and milk and blend until the mixture is frothy. Pour the mixture into a large glass, garnish with the whole mint leaf and add a straw. Drink immediately, chilled.

✳ *Bulgarian yoghurt is made from sheep's milk and characterised by the unique flavour, which is a result of the sheep grazing in herb-filled pastures. It is starting to become more widely available, but can be substituted with plain yoghurt if you can't find it.*

cakes

and desserts

cakes
and desserts

0% CHEESECAKE
IT MYLK–STYLE

makes 12 portions
preparation time 30 minutes (+ overnight draining time)
cooking time 1 hour 15 minutes
resting time 1 hour
refrigeration time overnight + 35 minutes

biscuit base
65 g (2¼ oz/½ cup) OAT BRAN
40 g (1½ oz/⅓ cup) CORNFLOUR
(CORNSTARCH)
1½ TEASPOONS BAKING POWDER
4 g ASPARTAME
1 VANILLA BEAN, SEEDS SCRAPED
120 g (4¼ oz) FAT-FREE PETIT-SUISSE CHEESE
OR QUARK ✷

cheesecake filling
2 kg (4 lb 8 oz) FAT-FREE YOGHURT
1 kg (2 lb 4 oz) FAT-FREE FAISSELLE CHEESE ✷
200 ml (7 fl oz) AGAVE SYRUP
5 EGGS
1 VANILLA BEAN, SEEDS SCRAPED
300 ml (10½ fl oz) LEMON JUICE

passionfruit jelly
300 ml (10½ fl oz) ORANGE JUICE, STRAINED
75 ml (2¼ fl oz) AGAVE SYRUP
4 g AGAR-AGAR
4 PASSIONFRUIT

equipment
24 cm (9½ inch) SPRING-FORM CAKE TIN,
6.5 cm (2½ inches) DEEP

✷ *See page 14.*

STRAINING
The day before, put the yoghurt and faisselle cheese in a colander lined with muslin (cheesecloth) and set it over a bowl. Let it drain overnight in the refrigerator. Only a firm paste should remain.

BISCUIT BASE
Combine the oat bran, cornflour, baking powder, aspartame and the vanilla seeds. Add the petit-suisse, combine until the mixture forms a ball and rest for 15 minutes in the refrigerator. Preheat the oven to 175°C (325°F/Gas 3). Line the base of the tin with a circle of baking paper. Place the mixture between two sheets of baking paper and roll out into a circle. When it's the same size as the base of the tin, remove the top sheet of paper and turn the circle over into the tin. Remove the second sheet of paper and press the mixture into the base. It should not go up the sides. Bake in the oven for 15 minutes.

CHEESECAKE FILLING
Mix together the strained yoghurt and faisselle cheese. Add the agave syrup and mix, then add the eggs one by one, whisking well. Add the vanilla seeds and the lemon juice. Reduce the oven to 150°C (300°F/Gas 2). Pour the cheesecake mixture over the biscuit base and return to the oven for 1 hour. Place a baking tray on a lower shelf to catch any drops. Let the cheesecake cool for about 1 hour in the turned-off oven with the door closed. Once cooled, cover the cheesecake with plastic wrap and refrigerate overnight.

PASSIONFRUIT JELLY
Bring the orange juice, agave syrup and agar-agar to the boil in a saucepan, stirring constantly. Cut the passionfruit in half and scoop out the pulp. Remove the saucepan from the heat, add the passionfruit pulp and mix. Pour the jelly over the cheesecake, then refrigerate for 20 minutes. Remove the cake tin ring and serve chilled.

MARCEL'S VARIATIONS

Change the flavour of the jelly: for strawberry, use 500 g (1 lb 2 oz) strawberry coulis (see page 30) and 4 g agar-agar. For lemon, use 500 g lemon curd (see page 38) and 4 g agar-agar.

VANILLA AND PECAN SPECULAAS CHEESECAKE

serves 12
preparation time 30 minutes (+ 12 hours draining time, if needed)
cooking time 2 hours 20 minutes
resting time 1 hour
refrigeration time 8 to 12 hours

biscuit base

75 g (2½ oz/¾ cup) PECANS, PLUS EXTRA TO SERVE
(OPTIONAL)
200 g (7 oz) SPECULAAS BISCUITS (COOKIES)
60 g (2¼ oz) LIGHTLY SALTED BUTTER
50 g (1¾ oz/⅓ cup) PLAIN (ALL-PURPOSE) FLOUR

filling

1.2 kg (2 lb 10 oz) LABNE OR
ABOUT 2.5 kg (5 lb 8 oz) FARMHOUSE OR
THICK GREEK YOGHURT
200 g (7 oz) CRÈME FRAÎCHE (40% DAIRY FAT)
5 EGGS
165 g (5¾ oz/¾ cup) SUGAR
50 ml (1¾ fl oz) MAPLE SYRUP
2 VANILLA BEANS, SEEDS SCRAPED
1 PINCH SALT

equipment

24 cm (9½ inch) SPRING-FORM CAKE TIN,
6.5 cm (2½ inches) DEEP

STRAINING

If you are using yoghurt in your cake filling, put the yoghurt in a colander lined with muslin (cheesecloth) and set it over a bowl. Let it drain overnight in the refrigerator. You should be left with 1.2 kg (2 lb 10 oz) of fairly firm fresh yoghurt cheese.

BISCUIT BASE

Preheat the oven to 180°C (350°F/Gas 4). Roast the pecans: spread them out on a baking tray lined with baking paper and place in the oven for 10 minutes. Roughly chop the pecans and speculaas with a knife. Melt the butter. Combine the speculaas, pecans, flour and melted butter. Press the mixture firmly into the base of the tin, and bake for 12 minutes.

FILLING

Lightly whisk the labne or yoghurt cheese with the crème fraîche. Mix in the whole eggs, one by one, then add the sugar, maple syrup, vanilla seeds and salt. Whisk this mixture together, pour it over the biscuit base in the tin, and return to the oven to cook for 5 minutes. After that, turn the oven down to 150°C (300°F/Gas 2) and cook for a further 55 minutes. The cheesecake should be firm around the edge with a little wobble in the centre. Leave to cool for another hour in the turned-off oven. Take it out and let it cool completely before putting it in the refrigerator. Remove from the spring-form tin the next day, decorate with pecans, if desired, and serve.

MARCEL'S CULTURE FLASH: WHAT IS LABNE?

Labne (or labneh) is a fresh cheese made from strained fermented milk. It looks like a thick fromage blanc. A speciality of Middle Eastern and North African cuisine, it is usually served at breakfast. Lightly salted with a drizzle of olive oil, it is served with bread, tomato, radishes … You can buy it in Middle Eastern grocery stores.

PEAR-CARAMEL CHEESECAKE

serves 12
preparation time 30 minutes (+ 12 hours draining time, if needed)
cooking time 2 hours 35 minutes
resting time 1 hour
refrigeration time 8 to 12 hours

biscuit base
75 g (2½ oz/¾ cup) PECANS
200 g (7 oz) SPECULAAS BISCUITS
60 g (2¼ oz) LIGHTLY SALTED BUTTER
50 g (1¾ oz/⅓ cup) PLAIN (ALL-PURPOSE) FLOUR

filling
1.2 kg (2 lb 10 oz) LABNE OR
ABOUT 2.5 kg (5 lb 8 oz) FARMHOUSE OR
THICK GREEK YOGHURT ✳
200 g (7 oz) CRÈME FRAÎCHE (40% DAIRY FAT)
5 EGGS
165 g (5¾ oz/¾ cup) SUGAR
50 ml (1½ fl oz) MAPLE SYRUP
1 VANILLA BEAN, SEEDS SCRAPED
1 PINCH SALT

pears
3 PEARS
2 TABLESPOONS CASTER (SUPERFINE) SUGAR

equipment
24 cm (9½ inch) SPRING-FORM CAKE TIN,
6.5 cm (2½ inches) DEEP

✳ *See Marcel's culture flash on page 138. Farmhouse yoghurt refers to yoghurt that has been made by small suppliers, such as farm shops, rather than mass-produced.*

STRAINING

If you are using yoghurt, put the yoghurt in a colander lined with muslin (cheesecloth) and set it over a bowl. Let it drain overnight in the refrigerator. You should be left with 1.2 kg (2 lb 10 oz) of fairly firm fresh yoghurt cheese.

BISCUIT BASE

Preheat the oven to 180°C (350°F/Gas 4). Roast the pecans: spread them out on a baking tray lined with baking paper and place in the oven for 10 minutes. Roughly chop the pecans and speculaas with a knife. Melt the butter. Combine the speculaas, pecans, flour and melted butter. Press the mixture firmly in the base of the tin and bake for 12 minutes.

CARAMELISED PEARS

Peel the pears and cut them into cubes. Heat the pear and sugar in a frying pan over a medium heat and let them caramelise until the pears are very soft.

FILLING

Lightly whisk the labne or yoghurt cheese with the crème fraîche. Mix in the whole eggs, one by one. Add the sugar, maple syrup, vanilla seeds and salt and whisk the mixture together. Arrange the pears over the biscuit base in the tin, pour over the filling, and cook for 5 minutes, then turn the oven down to 150°C (300°F/Gas 2) and cook for a further 55 minutes. The cheesecake should be firm around the edge with a slight wobble in the middle. Leave to cool for another hour in the turned-off oven. Take it out of the oven and let it cool completely before putting in the refrigerator. Remove from the spring-form tin the next day and serve.

MINI CHEESECAKES
NO-BAKE

makes 8
preparation time 30 minutes
cooking time 10 to 12 minutes
resting time 1 hour
cooling time 15 minutes
refrigeration time 6 hours

filling
350 ml (12 fl oz) THICKENED (WHIPPING) CREAM
720 g (1 lb 9 oz) CREAM CHEESE (SUCH AS PHILADELPHIA)
1 VANILLA BEAN, SEEDS SCRAPED
180 g (6 oz) RAW (DEMERARA) SUGAR
1 LEMON

breton shortbread biscuits
110 g (3¾ oz/¾ cup) PLAIN (ALL-PURPOSE) FLOUR
2 PINCHES SALT
2 PINCHES BAKING POWDER
1 VANILLA BEAN, SEEDS SCRAPED
90 g (3¼ oz) UNSALTED BUTTER, SOFTENED
75 g (2½ oz/⅓ cup) SUGAR
2 EGG YOLKS

equipment
8 PASTRY RINGS, 8 cm (3¼ inches) ACROSS,
5 cm (2 inches) DEEP
ELECTRIC BEATER

METHOD
Place the beater attachments and a bowl for whipping the cream in the freezer for 10 minutes. Take the cream cheese out of the refrigerator 15 minutes before using, so it's easier to work with.

BRETON SHORTBREAD BISCUITS
Work the flour, salt, baking powder, vanilla seeds and butter, cut into small pieces, together with your hands until you have a coarse sandy texture. Add the sugar and rub it through. Make a well in the dough, put the egg yolks in it, cover with dough mixture and crush them with the palm of your hand. Cover with mixture again and repeat until the egg yolks are completely incorporated. Lightly flatten the ball of dough, cover with plastic wrap and set aside to rest for 1 hour in the refrigerator. Preheat the oven to 170°C (325°F/Gas 3). Take the dough out of the refrigerator and work it again to soften. Flour your work surface and rolling pin and roll out the dough to a thickness of 1 cm (½ inch). Make circles using the rings and place each biscuit, still inside its ring, on a baking tray lined with baking paper. Bake in the oven for 10–12 minutes. Allow to cool for 15 minutes.

FILLING
Whip the cream in the chilled bowl and set aside in the refrigerator. In another bowl, use the electric beater to beat together the cream cheese, the vanilla seeds, sugar, and the juice and grated zest of the lemon. Fold in the whipped cream using a spatula. Divide the filling between the biscuits, still in their rings, then refrigerate for 6 hours. Remove the rings from around the mini cheesecakes and serve chilled.

CHEF MARCEL'S PRESENTATION TIP

You can finely grate some lime zest on the mini cheesecakes, top with a thin layer of lemon or yuzu curd (see pages 38 and 40), or a berry coulis (see page 30).

LITTLE YOGHURT CAKES
WITH PRALINE + HAZELNUTS

makes 8 cakes
preparation time 30 minutes
cooking time 20 minutes

50 g (1¾ oz) LIGHTLY SALTED BUTTER
110 g (3¾ oz/½ cup) SUGAR
100 g (3½ oz/¾ cup) PLAIN (ALL-PURPOSE) FLOUR
50 g (1¾ oz/½ cup) ALMOND MEAL
2 TEASPOONS BAKING POWDER
50 g (1¾ oz) CRUSHED PRALINE (STORE-BOUGHT
OR FROM RECIPE ON PAGE 90)
50 g (1¾ oz/⅓ cup) TOASTED HAZELNUTS, SKINNED
125 g (4½ oz) NATURAL YOGHURT
2 EGGS

equipment
8 x 80 ml (2½ fl oz/⅓ cup) CAPACITY MUFFIN
MOULDS, 5 cm (2 inches) ACROSS BASE

METHOD
Preheat the oven to 180°C (350°F/Gas 4). Lightly grease the muffin moulds with butter. Melt the butter and keep it at room temperature. Mix the sugar, sifted flour, almond meal and baking powder together in a bowl. Melt the praline over a low heat. Remove from the heat, add the hazelnuts and mix with a spatula. Beat together the yoghurt, eggs and melted butter. Once the mixture is smooth, add the dry ingredients and hazelnut praline, breaking it up, if needed. Mix them through with the spatula for a few seconds to blend into the batter.

COOKING
Pour into the muffin moulds. Bake in the oven for 20 minutes, or until cooked and golden brown. Cool in the tins for a few minutes before removing to a wire rack to cool completely.

YOGHURT CAKE
APPLE–WALNUT–CRANBERRY

makes about 12 portions
preparation time 30 minutes
cooking time 55 minutes
cooling time 30 minutes

110 g (3¾ oz) LIGHTLY SALTED BUTTER, SOFTENED
110 g (3¾ oz/½ cup) SUGAR
2 EGGS
150 g (5½ oz/1 cup) PLAIN (ALL-PURPOSE) FLOUR
2 TEASPOONS BAKING POWDER
2 SMALL APPLES (PREFERABLY GRANNY SMITH),
PEELED, CORED AND GRATED
55 g (2 oz/⅓ cup) DRIED CRANBERRIES
100 g (3½ oz) NATURAL YOGHURT
50 g (1¾ oz) CHOPPED WALNUTS

equipment
21 x 9 cm (8¼ x 3½ inch) LOAF (BAR) TIN
ELECTRIC BEATER

METHOD
Preheat the oven to 180°C (350°F/Gas 4). Lightly grease the loaf tin. Cream the butter and sugar with the electric beater. Add the eggs and mix them with electric beater on a low speed. Add the flour and baking powder, sifted together, and mix in with a spatula. In another bowl, mix together the grated apple, cranberries, yoghurt and chopped walnuts, then combine the two mixtures.

COOKING
Pour the batter into the loaf tin. Bake for 15 minutes in the oven, then for 40 minutes at 160°C (315°F/Gas 2–3). Cool in the tin for 10 minutes before turning out onto a wire rack to cool completely.

GÂTEAU AU FROMAGE BLANC

serves 12
preparation time 45 minutes
resting time 1 hour
cooking time 1 hour 45 minutes
resting time 1 hour
refrigeration time 6 hours

sweet shortcrust pastry

180 g (6 oz) UNSALTED BUTTER, SOFTENED
125 g (4½ oz/1 cup) ICING (CONFECTIONERS')
SUGAR
35 g (1¼ oz/⅓ cup) ALMOND MEAL
1 WHOLE EGG + 1 YOLK
1 PINCH SALT
300 g (10½ oz/2 cups) PLAIN (ALL-PURPOSE) FLOUR

filling

750 g (1 lb 10 oz) FROMAGE BLANC OR QUARK ✳
220 g (7¾ oz/1 cup) SUGAR
2 VANILLA BEANS, SEEDS SCRAPED
40 g (1½ oz/⅓ cup) CORNFLOUR (CORNSTARCH)
150 ml (5 fl oz) THIN (POURING) CREAM
3 EGGS, SEPARATED

equipment

24 cm (9½ inch) SPRING-FORM CAKE TIN,
6.5 cm (2½ inches) DEEP
ELECTRIC BEATER

✳ *See page 14.*

SWEET SHORTCRUST PASTRY

Put the butter in a bowl with the icing sugar, and beat with the electric beater until the mixture is creamy. Add the almond meal, the whole egg and egg yolk, the salt and, to finish, stir in the sifted flour. Knead until you have a smooth dough. Form into a ball, wrap in plastic wrap and let it rest for at least 1 hour at room temperature. Line the base of the cake tin with a circle of baking paper. Place the pastry mixture between two sheets of baking paper and roll it out into a circle. When the circle is the same size as the base of the tin, remove the top sheet of paper and turn the circle over into the tin, centring it. Remove the second sheet of baking paper and trim the excess base mixture using a small knife: the base should not go up the sides.

FILLING

Preheat the oven to 140°C (275°F/Gas 1). Mix the fromage blanc with 150 g (5½ oz) of the sugar, vanilla seeds, cornflour and cream. Incorporate the egg yolks. Beat the egg whites to firm peaks using the electric beater with the remaining sugar, then fold them into the mixture using a spatula, taking care not to deflate them. Pour the filling mixture over the base and smooth the surface with a flexible spatula. Place the cake on a rack in the bottom of the oven and bake for 1 hour 45 minutes, then let it cool for about 1 hour in the turned-off oven, without opening the door. Take the cake out of the oven and turn it over onto a wire rack without unmoulding it. Refrigerate for at least 6 hours. Remove the cake tin ring, turn it back over onto a round plate and serve.

DOUBLE VANILLA YOGHURT CUPCAKES

makes 12 cupcakes
preparation time 30 minutes
cooking time 20 minutes
refrigeration time 30 minutes

cupcakes

3 SMALL EGGS
150 g (5½ oz/⅔ cup) CASTER (SUPERFINE) SUGAR
2 TEASPOONS VANILLA SUGAR✳
100 g (3½ oz) NATURAL YOGHURT
125 ml (4 fl oz/½ cup) NEUTRAL OIL
200 g (7 oz/1⅓ cups) PLAIN (ALL-PURPOSE) FLOUR
3 TEASPOONS BAKING POWDER
PINCH FINE SALT

mascarpone icing

200 g (7 oz) MASCARPONE CHEESE
60 g (2¼ oz/½ cup) ICING
(CONFECTIONERS') SUGAR
1 VANILLA BEAN, SEEDS SCRAPED
2–3 DROPS FOOD COLOURING
OF YOUR CHOICE

equipment

12 x 80 ml (2½ fl oz/⅓ cup) CAPACITY MUFFIN
MOULDS, 5 cm (2 inches) ACROSS BASE
ELECTRIC BEATER
PIPING (ICING) BAG AND STAR NOZZLE

✳ *The recipe for this is on page 106.*

CUPCAKES

Preheat the oven to 180°C (350°F/Gas 4). Separate the egg whites and yolks. Beat the egg yolks and sugars in a mixing bowl with the electric beater until they become pale and creamy, then add the yoghurt and oil. Add the flour and baking powder, sifted together, and mix until you have a smooth batter. In a separate bowl, beat the egg whites to soft peaks with a pinch of salt using the cleaned electric beater. Fold them gently into the batter with a spatula, being careful not to deflate them. Butter the muffin moulds and fill each one to two-thirds full with batter. Bake in the oven for about 20 minutes. Take them out of the oven, leave them to cool in the tin for a few minutes and then unmould. Place the cupcakes onto a wire rack to cool completely.

ICING

Beat the mascarpone with the icing sugar and vanilla seeds with the electric beater until the mixture is completely smooth, then incorporate the food colouring. Cover with plastic wrap and set aside in the fridge for about 30 minutes.

ASSEMBLY

Using a spatula, fill the piping bag (nozzle attached) with mascarpone icing and decorate the cupcakes.

LEMON YOGHURT CUPCAKES

makes 12 cupcakes
preparation time 30 minutes
cooking time 20 minutes
refrigeration time 30 minutes

cupcakes

1 SMALL LEMON
3 SMALL EGGS
165 g (5¾ oz/¾ cup) CASTER (SUPERFINE) SUGAR
100 g (3½ oz) NATURAL YOGHURT
125 ml (4 fl oz/½ cup) NEUTRAL OIL
200 g (7 oz/1⅓ cups) PLAIN (ALL-PURPOSE) FLOUR
3 TEASPOONS BAKING POWDER
PINCH FINE SALT

mascarpone icing

160 g (5½ oz) MASCARPONE CHEESE
40 g (1½ oz/⅓ cup) ICING (CONFECTIONERS')
SUGAR
GRATED ZEST OF ½ LEMON
1½ TEASPOONS LEMON JUICE
POPPY SEEDS, TO SPRINKLE

equipment

12 x 80 ml (2½ fl oz/⅓ cup) CAPACITY MUFFIN
MOULDS, 5 cm (2 inches) ACROSS BASE
ELECTRIC BEATER
PIPING (ICING) BAG AND STAR NOZZLE

CUPCAKES

Preheat the oven to 180°C (350°F/Gas 4). Zest the lemon using a fine grater. Separate the egg whites and yolks. Beat the egg yolks and sugar in a bowl using the electric beaters until they become pale and creamy, then add the lemon zest, yoghurt and oil. Add the sifted flour and baking powder and mix until you have a smooth batter. In a separate bowl, beat the egg whites to soft peaks with a pinch of salt using the cleaned electric beater. Fold them gently into the batter with a spatula, being careful not to deflate them. Butter the muffin moulds and fill each two-thirds full with batter. Bake in the oven for about 20 minutes. Take them out of the oven, let them cool in the tin for a few minutes and then unmould. Place the cupcakes onto a wire rack to cool completely.

ICING

Beat together the mascarpone, icing sugar, lemon zest and juice with the electric beater until you have a completely smooth mixture. Cover with plastic wrap and refrigerate for about 30 minutes.

ASSEMBLY

Using a spatula, fill the piping bag (nozzle attached) with the mascarpone icing and decorate the cupcakes. Decorate with thin strips of lemon zest and the poppy seeds.

RICE PUDDING WITH YOGHURT

serves 6
preparation time 10 minutes
cooking time 35 minutes
cooling time 20 minutes
refrigeration time 2 hours

1 litre (35 fl oz/4 cups) MILK
110 g (3¾ oz/½ cup) SUGAR, PLUS
2 TEASPOONS EXTRA
1 VANILLA BEAN
140 g (5 oz/⅔ cup) SHORT-GRAIN PUDDING RICE
120 g (4¼ oz) NATURAL YOGHURT

equipment
6 EARTHENWARE YOGHURT POTS

METHOD

Pour the milk into a heavy-based saucepan and add the 110 g of sugar and vanilla bean, split in half lengthways. Bring to a bare simmer over a medium heat, stirring regularly with a wooden spoon. Add the rice, reduce the heat to low, cover and cook for 30 minutes, stirring occasionally until the rice is cooked. Remove from the heat and let cool for about 20 minutes. Remove the vanilla bean. Whisk the yoghurt with the 2 extra teaspoons of sugar and mix in to the rice pudding. Divide the mixture between the yoghurt pots and refrigerate for at least 2 hours before serving.

MARCEL'S ADVICE

For rice pudding purists, serve the pudding as is; for others, you can add pieces of fresh fruit, caramel sauce or berry coulis (see page 30), depending on the season.

FROMAGE BLANC MOUSSE
WITH RASPBERRIES + SPECULAAS

serves 6
preparation time 20 minutes
cooking time 5 minutes
refrigeration time 4 hours

250 ml (9 fl oz/1 cup) THIN (POURING) CREAM
500 g (1 lb 2 oz) FROMAGE BLANC (20% DAIRY FAT)
OR QUARK ✳
4 g AGAR-AGAR
200 g (7 oz) SUGAR
250 g (9 oz/2 cups) RASPBERRIES
6 SPECULAAS BISCUITS (COOKIES)

equipment
ELECTRIC BEATER
6 SMALL GLASSES

METHOD

Pour the cream into a freezer-safe bowl and place in the freezer for about 10 minutes. Take it out and beat with the electric beater to make chantilly cream. Place a heaped tablespoon of fromage blanc and the agar-agar into a small saucepan, then bring to the boil over a medium heat, stirring constantly. Pour the mixture into a large bowl, add the rest of the fromage blanc and sugar, mix and fold in the whipped cream. Divide the mixture between six small glasses and refrigerate for at least 4 hours. Rinse the raspberries. Roughly chop the speculaas biscuits.

ASSEMBLY

Take the small glasses of mousse out of the refrigerator. Place a few raspberries on each and sprinkle with the crumbled biscuits.

✳ *See page 14.*

156

RECIPE INDEX

IT MYLK IN PARIS

SHOP 15 Rue de l'Ancienne Comédie, 75006 Paris
KIOSK 1 Place Suzanne Valadon, 75018 Paris
GALERIES LAFAYETTE 48 Boulevard Haussman, 6th floor, 75009 Paris
CHARLES DE GAULLE AIRPORT Terminal 2 A-C
www.itmylk.fr

THANK YOUS

To Marcel, who, with one look, can make you forget everything and laugh.

To JOUR, our official kale supplier.

To Matthieu, for the buzz he's going to create around this book.

To our parents, who gave us the courage to have a go and the confidence to never give up.

To Laura and Marie, for their wonderful recipe ideas.

To Gabrielle, for THE it mylk frozen yoghurt recipe.

To David and Sabrina, whose eyes and hands made this book.

To Camille and Marine, who are wildly talented.

To Mickaël, who took care of the day-to-day.

To the cows at Viltain farm, to *Benoît*, who was the first to believe in us,

and to Franck, who delivers to us each Monday with passion.

To our friends, who have followed the it mylk adventure from the beginning and who give us encouragement every day.

To the whole it mylk team, whose routine has been turned upside down during these intense weeks of work.

To Groupe SEB, for its yoghurt makers, blenders and ice-cream makers.

To Pauline and Rosemarie, who started this mad project.

To our shareholders, without whom nothing would be possible.

To all those who have had faith in us since the beginning of the it mylk adventure
and who support us every day with their warm and very useful advice.

To all those who "like" all our Facebook® posts.

To all those who send us benchmark photos from the four corners of the planet.

To the it Twingo, which has never really let us down.

To all those we've met along the way and who have made us love our jobs.

To all the other young entrepreneurs who made us understand that anything was possible.

To Édouard, for his sharp but always well-informed advice.

To Thomas, thank you for... **EVERYTHING**.

Finally, *to all those* who are going to buy one, twenty-five or fifty copies of this book and give it to all of their loved ones.
To everyone, **MERCI!**

SUPPLIERS

MERCI 111 Boulevard Beaumarchais 75003 Paris
BONTON 5 Boulevard des Filles du Calvaire 75003 Paris / 82 Rue de Grenelle 75007 Paris
UP UTILE ET PRATIQUE 14 Rue Froissart 75003 Paris
HEMA 118 Rue Rambuteau 75001 Paris and *HEMA.fr*

First published by Hachette Livre (Marabout) in 2013
Published in 2014 by Murdoch Books, an imprint of Allen & Unwin.

Murdoch Books Australia
83 Alexander Street
Crows Nest NSW 2065
Phone: +61 (0) 2 8425 0100
Fax: +61 (0) 2 9906 2218
www.murdochbooks.com.au
info@murdochbooks.com.au

Murdoch Books UK
Erico House, 6th Floor
93–99 Upper Richmond Road
Putney, London SW15 2TG
Phone: +44 (0) 20 8785 5995
www.murdochbooks.co.uk
info@murdochbooks.co.uk

For Corporate Orders & Custom Publishing contact
Noel Hammond, National Business Development Manager, Murdoch Books Australia

Publisher: Corinne Roberts
Photographer: David Japy
Stylist: Sabrina Fauda-Rôle
Graphic design: M/B(wearemb.com)
Illustrations: Alix Baron
Food editor and testing: Michelle Earl
Translator: Melissa McMahon
Editor: Gordana Trifunovic
Editorial manager: Katie Bosher
Production: Karen Small

Text and Design © Hachette Livre (Marabout) 2013

A cataloguing-in-publication entry is available from the catalogue of the National Library of Australia at www.nla.gov.au.

A catalogue record for this book is available from the British Library.

Colour reproduction by Splitting Image, Clayton, Victoria.

Printed by 1010 Printing International Limited, China.

IMPORTANT: Those who might be at risk from the effects of salmonella poisoning (the elderly, pregnant women, young children and those suffering from immune deficiency diseases) should consult their doctor with any concerns about eating raw eggs.

OVEN GUIDE: You may find cooking times vary depending on the oven you are using. For fan-forced ovens, as a general rule, set the oven temperature to 20°C (35°F) lower than indicated in the recipe.

MEASURES GUIDE: We have used 20 ml (4 teaspoon) tablespoon measures. If you are using a 15 ml (3 teaspoon) tablespoon add an extra teaspoon of the ingredient for each tablespoon specified.